Circles of Sisterhood

A BOOK DISCUSSION GROUP GUIDE
FOR WOMEN OF COLOR

● ● ● ● ● ● ● ● ● ● ● ● ● ● ● ●

Pat Neblett

HARLEM RIVER PRESS
NEW YORK
& LONDON

Published for Harlem River Press
by Writers and Readers Publishing, Inc.
P.O. Box 461 Village Station
New York, NY 10014

Writers and Readers Limited
c/o Airlift Book Company
8, The Arena
Mollison Avenue
Enfield EN37NJ
England

Editor: Patricia A. Allen
Book Production: Pauline Neuwirth Associates
Cover Design: Terrie Dunkelberger
Cover Art ©: Kreshaun McKinney

Library of Congress Cataloging-in Publication Data
Neblett, Pat.
    Circles of sisterhood : a book discussion group guide for women of
color / Pat Neblett.
      p.   cm.
    ISBN 0-86316-245-2
    1. Group reading—United States.   2. Afro-American women—
Education—Reading.   I. Title.
LC6851.N43   1996
374' .22—dc20   96-41222
                                                                CIP

0 9 8 7 6 5 4 3 2 1

Manufactured in the United States of America

Dedication

This book is dedicated to my mom, with whom I wrote my first poem; to my wonderful children Touré and Meika for their encouragement and creative advice; to all of the members of the Black Women's Literary Guild, my book dicscussion group for their inspiration; to Sisters With a Pen, my writers group, for their constructive criticism; to Marie Brown, my agent, who saw potential in my proposal; Patricia Allen, my editor, who didn't give up on me and brought the book into fruition; and to my very own circle of sisterhood: Barbara Cruz, Carole (just call me Lisa) Alkins, Gert Cowan, Katherine Kennedy, Roz Johnson, Marva Nathan, Martha Welch, and Liz Woodly, for their friendship and support. Most of all, the book is dedicated to my very best friend, my husband Roy, who makes all my dreams come true.

Acknowledgments

I'd like to thank librarians everywhere, especially Eileen at the Milton Library, who graciously contributed to this project.

$\mathcal{T}able\ of\ \mathcal{C}ontents$

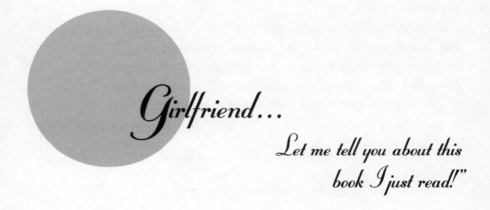

Girlfriend...

*Let me tell you about this
book I just read!"*

That's me on the phone after I've read a good book. Maybe it's you too. Sometimes I get so excited about what I read that I will tell everyone I know, even people I've just met. Early on, before I began discussion groups, I remember feeling very frustrated that most of my book conversations happened over the telephone. Most of the time the "girlfriend" hadn't read the book, and by the time she did, I'd moved on to something else. I remembered thinking how nice it would be if a group of us "girlfriends" got together and just talked about books. That was my incentive in starting my first group. If you're like me and go crazy when you don't have a book to read and love the idea of a girlfriends book club, but are not sure how to get started, then *Circles of Sisterhood: A Book Discussion Group Guide for Women of Color* is for you. It's a concise, step-by-step guide to everything you need to know to start a book discussion group, including book selection, author appearances, and how to handle readings that provoke conflict. You'll also learn how to sustain the interest in the members for the group and how to enhance an existing group. You'll even learn how to know which books are best for discussion, and what's being published in the marketplace.

I absolutely love to read. Always have. I always have a book with me, even when I go to the movies. You may think that's a little extreme, but you'd be surprised how much you can read before the previews start. Between chitchat with my husband, while the movie trivia is playing, and before the lights go down, I can usually put away a couple pages. I've actually seen a couple of other

• • • • • • • • • • • • • • •

The book discussion group has

changed my life. I've found new

friends, new authors, lots of laughs,

and some serious discussion.

— Martha Welch

• • • • • • • • • • • • • • •

women doing the same thing. I also like to relax with a book in a hot tub briming with bubbles. Whenever I have a book that I can't seem to start, I'm able to do so when I'm in the tub.

More and more these days, because of the demands on my time, I seem to rely on books on tape. *Not* as a substitute for reading; there is no substitute for actually reading the book, or holding one in your hands. I'm in my car a lot, and listening to books on tapes is a great way to make use of that time. Listening to books on tape, especially those books read by the author, allows me to hear the cadence and inflections that the author intended when she or he

wrote the book, but that I may not be able to "hear" what I'm reading. This is especially critical for me when a book is written in
dialect. If the book on tape is interesting, then I'll look forward to
the book. Rarely have I been disappointed. Neither has my group.

My love of reading started with my mother, who read a lot and
still does. As a child I would ask for Christmas toys from the Sears
& Roebuck catalogue and for books. I don't remember the toys, but
I do remember the books. My favorite was *The Secret Garden* by
Mary Francis Burnatt. African Americans (and most likely other
people of color) of my generation didn't have the priviledge of
reading books that portrayed positive images of our children. Back
then, we never saw ourselves in books. In fact, such books are a relatively recent phenonmenon. I've often believed that my insatiable
appetite for Black authors, history, and historical fiction have very
much to do with this deprivation. Children don't realize how much
better it is today.

My mother and I became engaged then, and still often do, in discussion about books. We were, I realize now, a literary group of
two, and I mean literary in the strictest sense of the word. Back
then, literary socities, as they were often called, were usually
encumbered with a social or political agenda. Today, reading
groups often accomodate issues beyond books too, like equality in
the corporate world and other women's rights issues.

The publishing industry changed with the Civil Rights
Movement of the 1960s. Not only was there a focus on children's
books, but indeed on all kinds of books emphasizing the needs of
people of color. Immediately following the Movement, books portraying positive images of African Americans were mass-pro-
duced. This trend lasted for about ten years, then lost momentum
for two reasons: (1) With the exception of the very few books
appearing on "Best Seller" lists, an overwhelming majority of
books by people of color go unknown by the vast majority of people and are difficult to locate; (2) books by people of color have a
"short" shelf life. That is, if they don't sell quickly, then they're in

the remainder bins. Until the '90s, publishers not wanting to risk publishing books that would have a short shelf life published the same, few Black writers who had proven themselves. While this was great for elite and established writers, it did little to encourage new authors.

The modern renaissance of readers, and books published, is thought by many to have begun in 1982 with Alice Walker's Pulitzer Prize winning book *The Color Purple*, with a renewed interest in the book coming after the movie was produced. Readers, representing a multitude of ethnicities, wanting well-written literature, bought books by Toni Morrison, Alice Walker, Amy Tan, and Laura Esquivel propelling these authors to the top of the charts. The overwhelming success of books such as *Song of Solomon*, *The Color Purple*, *The Joy Luck Club*, and *Like Water for Chocolate* are evidence that well-written, accessibly interesting, entertaining books sell, no matter who writes them. But it was Terry McMillan's *Waiting to Exhale* that convinced publisher's that people of color buy books if there is something to sell. It goes without saying that people of color have known all along that if there are books about us, we'll buy them. Of course, Blacks alone didn't catapult *Waiting to Exhale* off the charts and onto the the big screen, but without us, the book's success is doubtful.

Today, books portraying people of color are written in every genre, from romance to detective novels, from autobiographies to science fiction; they're even being serialized in hard cover. In fact, they're being published faster than we can read them. However, the question of quality more than quantity now becomes a concern. Consumers must be willing to accept the responsibility to insist that these books are of a high of quality. This is imperative if we are to continue the legacy left us by the authors of *Native Son*, *Invisible Man*, and *Their Eyes Were Watching God*, books written over forty years ago, that have endured the test of time, and like Wright, Ellison, and Hurston, leave us with the gift of a literary legacy.

Having the luxury of hundreds of titles available that reflect a diversity of genres is a "novel" experience for people of color. Being able to discuss books in book discussion groups is also a novel experience. So, too, are discussions of ethnically themed books among people of the same ethnic group. Some would describe it as a very spiritual, very satisfying experience.

Nurturers by nature, and hard workers by necessity, many women have felt the need to bond, especially with women like themselves. Since the earliest times, women have felt a need to join literary societies in order to connect with women with whom they share a cultural identity. Among Black women, there is a history of reading groups well over 150 years old. White women formed similar groups much earlier. (See Appendix: A Historical Look at Book Discussion Groups.) Literary societies, as they were often called, were frequently encumbered with a political agenda. Well-educated, middle-class white women might discuss suffrage. Black women, often educated and middle-class, might discuss abolition and civil rights. Men had their groups too, often with an ambition toward self-improvement. Just as women need to share their experiences with other women, women of color need to be in the company of their sisters—at least sometimes.

Typically, book discussion groups today don't usually have socio-economic qualifications, and very few are politically and/or socially restrictive, the exception being a Bible reading group or something similar. Reading groups are generally very inclusive, provided members share the same goals of the group. Some groups are for mystery lovers only; others may read only historical nonfiction. Still others may read only biographies. Many have multigenre interests.

Book discussion groups where members are all of the same ethnicity not only provide an opportunity to talk about books, but for some, they offer a much-needed support group. This is especially crucial today as many of us either live or work in environments that don't allow us to celebrate ourselves. Discussion groups provide contexts for making friends, networking, and talking about cultural issues. For women who use the excuse of "being too busy," groups force them to find the time to get out of the house and read. Reflecting on the value of being a member of the Saturday Eve's Book Club, in Kalamazoo, Michigan, Betty Boulding wrote:

> *My memories include books and authors, summer picnics, gracious meals in members' homes, [our] twentieth annversary, and inter- racting with women, and the community. Most of all, I remember the concerned and involved women who supported and helped me to become more than I had been.*

Beyond the personal impact book discussion groups have on individual lives, there is a great potential to affect the publishing industry. If book discussion groups across the country all read the same books within a years' time, it would be an impressive show of clout that would send a powerful economic message: that the ethnic market is one that should not be ignored.

A year after I founded the Black Women's Literary Guild, in 1991, the group was mentioned in an article in *American Visions*, and during the same period, I developed and wrote a book discus- sion group newlsetter focused on African American literature. I believe it was the first of its kind. Both publications reached women across the country, and I received many inquiries with the same question, "How do I start a book discussion group?" It was then that I realized there was a need for a formal book discussion group guide, and that I was, perhaps, the woman to do it.

Chapter 1

STARTING A BOOK
DISCUSSION GROUP

• • • • • • • • • • • • • • •

Being a member of

a women's book

discussion group has

given me the sisters

I never had.

—Barbara Cruz

Getting the Sisters Together...

First, you might want to ask yourself the question, "Why do I want to start a book discussion group?" If the answer is, "Because I like to read, and I like to talk about what I read," then you're halfway there. Desire is half of what's needed to start a group. The other half: an ability to organize and coordinate details and to arrange schedules. I asked and answered the question myself in 1991, when I formed the Black Women's Literary Guild (BWLG), and I haven't looked back since.

At the time, I'd never even been to a book discussion group and didn't really know what to do. But, using my innate organizational skills, I proceeded one step at a time, starting first with calling up all my book-loving friends. Bibliophiles are wonderful people, so knowing that they were behind me in my efforts to start a group, I was confident that, at the very least, discussion would be lively.

An opportunity for lively book discussion is pretty much all, at that time anyway, I thought a book discussion group was. I saw it simply as a more formalized effort of what my mother and I did when I was a child—-very casually talking about books together.

Gathering Friends

Contacting like-minded friends is the most obvious place to start. The Women's Culture Club/Literary Circle, in Detroit, Michigan, was founded with a few old college friends as its core group. Fact is, most groups that I'm in communication with started with friends. Having their support and knowing you have people to depend on for assistance is comforting. I discovered that all the women in my group were eager for the same reason I was: We really enjoyed one another's friendship. A discussion group gave us one more day together, another day to become even closer.

I asked each of the core members of my group for the name of a friend and invited everyone to an "Interest Meeting." I ended up with twenty-six members at that meeting, on what happened to be the hottest July evening in Boston's history.

Rosalind Oliphant, owner of *Folktales Bookstore* in Austin, Texas, reported that she hadn't planned to start a book discussion group until customers "kept asking about an opportunity to get together with others to discuss books." And both Hue-Man Experience, in Denver, and the Community Bookstore, in Baton Rouge, Louisiana, are the source for a couple of others groups that were started in response to their customers.

One of the most poignant letters that I received describing their beginning was from the PALM Society in Bloomfield, Connecticut, a discussion group founded in 1991.

> It all began one night after hearing Maya Angelou give a poetry reading in Lincoln Theater at the University of Hartford, where I was serving as associate dean of students. As Ms. Angelou likes to do, she shared many of her thoughts and feelings with the audience between her readings of both her own poetry and that of other

authors. It was truly an enjoyable and inspiring evening. At one point, she wondered aloud how many of us regularly read and talked about the works of Ralph Ellison, Zora Neale Hurston, James Baldwin, and Ernest Gaines.

Her question reminded me that I had organized and belonged to a book club when our family lived in Boston, and that I had missed the learning and fellowship since moving to Connecticut ten years before. Ms. Angelou's question seemed to be a clarion call for action.

A few days later, I made a phone call to two colleagues. I shared my thoughts with them regarding the possibility of starting a group which would be primarily devoted to an appreciation of the arts of the peoples of the African Diaspora, not only in poetry, but in music, literature, and the other arts as well. I thought of the PALM Society as an acronym for Poetry, Art, Literature, and Music. Also from Ms. Angelou's reading of Waring Cuny's poem, "No Images," it had occurred to me that if in the Society we could be figurative "palm trees," i.e., provide a collective space in which the various images of ourselves as depicted in the arts of our people could be viewed, studied and appreciated, the benefits to ourselves would be numerous and certain.

Both colleagues were highly enthusiastic, and we immediately began to explore the issue of an appropriate meeting space, i.e., hotel function room or other space, that would relieve members of the necessity of hosting meetings. After exploring, we agreed to request permission to use a University of Hartford facility, A.S.K. House, since we believed that what we were proposing was an easy fit with the University's Mission. Permission was granted, and the three of us met over lunch to plan the first meeting. Each of us agreed to invite several of our friends to attend an organizational meeting. Sixteen women attended.

From the Church, PTA, Fitness Club, etc.

You could post a note at your sports club, place a notice in the church bulletin, mention it at the PTA meeting, or at any other place you happen to be, including—if you live in an apartment building—the laundry room, mailroom, etc. The founder of one group that I heard from said that upon moving to a new neighborhood, she went door to door like the Avon Lady, soliciting interest in starting a group. She got three women on the first day. Just enough to start. That's right. As few as three can be the nucleus of a book discussion group. So don't wait for too many sisters or, if you wish, brothers. Once the word is out that you're going to start a book discussion group, prospective members will find you.

Just Between Us is comprised of employees of the U.S. Department of Labor, B.L.S., in Washington, D.C. Founder Lori Lewis says that the group was founded when: "She learned that co-workers were reading books individually and discussing them together informally."

By Chance Encounters

Books are a wonderful catalyst for bringing people together. In my pre-book discussion group days, I joined a large women's organization. Not knowing many people, and not knowing if I'd be accepted by one of the many cliques already in-place, using books as my security blanket, I'd take out one of the two or three books that I would carry in my tote bag and read until the meeting began.

Sooner or later, someone would say: "So, what are you reading?" or "I just read that book...." or "Did you read...?" I actually met a lot of people with similar interests this way.

Once, while I was waiting for my husband in Bloomingdales and, yes, reading a book, a woman asked what I was reading.

Mama, I said, by Terry McMillan. She suggested that I read Gloria Naylor's *Mama Day*. I thanked her for the recommendation. After reading the book, which I thoroughly enjoyed, I realized, too late, that she would have been great in my book club. So seize those opportunities to recruit. Spread the word. Get started!

The Interest Meeting

The Interest Meeting is the initial meeting, where it is decided just how your group is going to operate—how often it will meet, where, when, etc. If at all possible, arrange some of your favorite books in the meeting room. You might even ask friends to bring books too. Place them strategically around the room. This will give everyone something to talk about.

When prospective members arrive make sure that there are at least two people to greet them. It is important that everyone be introduced, and that people be made to feel comfortable immediately. Name tags go a long way in helping break the ice, as well as aiding the memory in time in need. I prefer the ones that say, "Hi, my name is," because they're much friendlier than blank ones.

If you can't get enough name tags in a variety of colors, mark two (or more, depending on size of group) with the same color. For example, mark two with red, another two with blue, etc. Instruct guests to seek out and interview anyone with the same color name tag or dot, asking her/him her profession, personal goals, interests, secret wishes, childhood nicknames, something funny that happened to her/him, etc. This "get acquainted" period should last no more than fifteen to twenty minutes, half-hour tops. Soon after, if you are the hostess, you should announce that the meeting will begin.

Once everyone is seated and comfortable, ask guests to stand and briefly introduce those with like name tags. Continue doing this until everyone has been introduced. Such exchanges are fun and less intimidating than when an individual is asked to introduce her/himself to the group. At one meeting, two people discovered they were distantly related.

In the book *The Serpent's Gift*, when the character Ruby died, her family didn't know about the hurt she'd carried. Far too often, a person goes out of our lives, and later we realize there was so much that we didn't know about them. This can be someone who you were close to, someone that you saw regularly.

Once a month members sit across from each other, yet some never get to know the others. If after several meetings you don't feel that members are getting involved with each other, I'd suggest a questionnaire. Make up a list of general questions, using, say, *TheSerpent's Gift* as a context, and asking each member to complete it by interviewing the person across from her, anyone other than a friend; if so, interview someone you don't know well. In the BWLG half the group are best friends, the other half are friends to varying degrees.

Sample Questionnaire From *(The Serpent's Gift)*

1. LaRue painted Selina's rocking chair yellow, a color he said was hers. What color would you claim for yourself?
2. If you had to mark time by the significance of events in your life, what things in the past twelve months you would have recorded?

3. Ruby had a recognizable moment of the week. What was your recognizable moment of the last week?
4. Your birth month?
5. Favorite times of the year?
6. Kinds of interest or activities enjoyed?
7. Favorite spots?
8. What kind of work do you do?
9. How many children do you have?
10. Are you married? Divorced? Never married? Significant other? Looking? Not Looking?
11. What one thing do you want to achieve this year?
12. Where is your favorite spot to think? If you could have one, single thing that you don't have, what would it be?
13. What are you willing to give up to attain it?
14. What smells trigger the most pleasant memories for you?
15. Why?
16. List of three good things in your life.
17. What two kinds of things, or thoughts, would you put into a keepsake jar?
18. LaRue asks Olive if she could become an animal, which would she choose? LaRue said he became a snake because a snake is a survivor, but most of all, when it gets finished with the skin it's wearing, it sheds it, crawling out of the past and into the future. If you could become an animal, which would you choose? Why?

I've found this a good way to begin the Interest Meeting; sharing why you wanted to create your book discussion group, then asking everyone to share what they hope to get from joining one. Don't be surprised if answers are basically the same. A few will say they're here because they want "to do something for me," and meeting with a reading group is a good way to spend their time. Others will say they love to read and want to have someone besides an uninterested husband, roommate, or baby to share their book-related thoughts with. Some may admit that they want to be encouraged to read books outside their comfort zone; to broaden their reading interests and to read books that they would not normally read if it weren't for an organized discussion group. Many women I've met joined a group because they needed an incentive to read. Whatever reason they have for being there, like you, they like books.

Also ask if anyone has been in a discussion group before. Anyone who has should be encouraged to share their previous experiences. Information from this knowledgable member is invaluable to you, especially if this is your first time putting together such a group. Your group can benefit by learning in advance the negatives and positives of operating a successful a group. Don't let this person go on, though, especially about negative things. Perhaps after this initial meeting, you can invite this person to lunch or for coffee and discuss in detail any bad experiences or situations that arose with the other group.

Ask each guest to share the titles of three to five books they've read or would like to read, along with a *brief* synopsis for the group. If there are more than ten people, you might want to ask for only one book title and synopsis. You'll quickly learn the type of books these prospective members read, plus you'll get a list of books for future reading. Before the meeting ends, have the group vote on books that interest them. If you don't have a number-one best seller that you're eager to read, you can decide to select the book with the highest score as the one you'll read for the first discussion meeting. If there's a tie for first, then the voting can go around just for those two or three books, until a decision is made. If more than half of your group has read the same book, you might want to select something that less than three-fourths of them have not read for your first official meeting. Later, when everyone is familiar with everyone else, you might go back to a title that the majority of the group has read.

Suggested Agenda for the Interest Meeting:

When to meet ... day of the week

Finding a day that's good for everyone is next to impossible. Get a consensus, a day that's best for most members; hopefully you won't lose interested members, but you should encourage them to come back if their schedule changes. Establishing a definite day and time works better than having to remember to notify members for each future meeting. If need be, you can send notices. During months with five weeks, I send postcard reminders. Some groups send reminder notices for each meeting. I did this for about a year until the third Monday at 6:30p.m. became as automatic a thing to remember as going to work.

Time to meet ...

The Myrtle Literary Guild, a book discussion group in West Newton, Massachusetts, likes to meet Sunday directly after church; but whether your group meets noontime at work, or right after work, mid-Saturday afternoon— the best time of day is the time that's best for the majority of members. There is no right day or time. For me, Saturday and Sunday are not good for BWLG (my group) activities, because those are the days I reserve to spend time with my husband. Since he plays tennis every night, evening meetings work best for me. Remember: *Your* schedule is the most important schedule.

Tardiness

The Interest Meeting is the time you need to set policy about punctuality. Unless impossible, you, the organizer or host should be notified that a member will be late. Some groups have a rule that after a specified number of late arrivals, the member is asked to leave. If the majority of the members agree that such action is necessary, then this should become, as indeed all rules, part of a handbook or member's rules and behavior, and passed out to each new member.

Attendance

Attendance requirements are crucial for small groups. Some groups state that if a member misses two consecutive meetings, that person will be asked to leave, to make room for someone else who is more committed. The question is, how structured do you want to be, and what are the circumstances under which a member who misses meetings will be excused? For instance, Dorothy, a member for six years, is pregnant and decides after giving birth to take six months off from the group. Should this be allowed? I think so. More likely, your members will think so too.

Summer or holiday meetings?

Many groups recess during the summer. But because I thought that continuity was important, the BWLG meets through the summer. December, on the other hand, is such a busy time that we decided to break for the holiday month. Even so, we do have a holiday party sometime between Christmas and the New Year, and I will during the month-long hiatus send a postcard to remind members of the next meeting date.

How long should discussions last?

Going over notices or business five to ten minutes prior to the meeting works better than after. Often, people have to leave before the meeting ends. I've found that just prior to the meeting, more people are present. On average, a book can be thoroughly discussed in about an hour, though count on two. You'll need about fifteen minutes to go over business or member-related news that has happened since the last meeting, or that will take place prior to the next meeting. The BWLG convenes at six-thirty, with the discussion starting *promptly* at seven, even if only three of the sixteen people expected have arrived. Because everyone is busy, it's important to start on time. Knowing that you start promptly is an incentive for people to make it on time and not to stroll in because the group starts any ole time. Also, members should be encouraged to be on time to avoid unnecessary interruptions. We will wait ten to fifteen minutes for the facilitator to arrive however; after that the group goes ahead, yes, even without the designated facilitator. (See Chapter 3, Facilitating) When she arrives, she takes over. In an emergency, you'll find that members will rise to the occasion. While it's possible to have a discussion in an emergency situation, without a facilitator, I wouldn't recommend it as an operating procedure. Only once, in my experience, did a facilitator not show. Even so, an animated discussion pursued. If you're in a similar situation, solicit for a volunteer, and if that doesn't work, designate someone.

How often to meet?

Most groups meet once a month. However, there are no set rules. If members' schedules are so busy that they can't possibly read one book a month, then meeting less often would be better. Whether you're going to meet every other month on Wednesday, or every third month on Tuesday, make a decision. The You Go Girl book group in Broadview, Illinois, meets quarterly. As unbelievable as it seems, I heard of one group that meets weekly, while another calls a meeting whenever a "good" book comes out.

Where to meet: homes, book store, library, etc.?

The coziest place to meet is usually thought to be a member's home. But all homes are not created equal. There are serious considerations to think about:

- Is the room where you'll meet adequate to accommodate the number of members expected? For comfort's sake, a large group in a small room is not necessarily a good idea. Members may be willing to volunteer their homes, but if their accomodations are inappropriate, tactfully discourage them.

- Is the member's home centrally located, or is it too far from most members? Driving an hour may be enjoyable on a beautiful Sunday afternoon, but after work, at night, when it is raining or snowing, the drive becomes a chore.

- If the meeting is to be held in an apartment, should you make arrangements with building security? The hostess will either have to provide a list of expected guests or be prepared to be contacted by the security whenever a guest arrives, in which case there will be repeated interruptions.

- Is there ample convenient parking near the meeting site? Do neighbors need to be advised that guests will be parking in front of their houses? Some people seem to think they own the space on the street in front of their house, and get upset looking out and seeing a strange car parked there. Such questions should be asked of the hostess of the prospective meeting place.

Remember to tell members where not to park, i.e., school or church parking lots, if there is a chance of getting a ticket or being towed.

- Is the meeting location quiet enough? Are there children, a husband, roommates, or someone who is ill and will need attention, or someone who will be cooking in the kitchen or will have the tv or stereo blasting loudly? Distractions can break ones train of thought.

- Are there pets? That cat or dog you love more than anything on earth may be the source of allergy or cause fear in others. Conversely, members should be asked not to bring animals to meetings. Bringing animals to another member's home is inconsiderate not only to the host but also to other members. Hosts should not be placed in the awkward position of saying no, so don't ask if you can bring your pet to a meeting.

- Are there other places to meet? If there is a more suitable meeting site, then pursue it. Comfort is your priority.

If it's inconvenient to meet at a member's home, check with the owner of a local bookstore. Many allow book groups to meet there after regular store hours, and many libraries have a private room that they'll let you use for a small fee.

My daughter recently saw four women involved in a serious book discussion at a Starbucks coffee shop. Because BWLG's discussions are far too animated, my group wouldn't be a good candidate to meet in a public space. For other groups, though—those that can maintain a sense of decorum—book store and/or coffee shops are ideal locations. I would suggest no more than six members if you can get a round table, and a maximum of four if the table is square. The configuration of the table is a consideration if everyone is to be heard.

If members all work in the same or nearby building, like the Bunch for Lunch, a coed group in Houston, Texas, you may decide to meet in the cafeteria or ask to use a board or conference room, like Just Between Us in Fredericksburg, Virginia. If you have to use a library or book store, this may determine the day and time of meetings.

Often, a community room in an apartment complex or an common room in a community building will be available.

Dues? How much? How often?

I'd strongly suggest collecting a fee to cover expenses. Mailings and copying notices throughout the year are costly. If you decide to have a newsletter, there will be additional expenses. Also, there's something about paying dues that give members a feeling of commitment. If dues collected are in excess of immediate expenses, that is, if you have money that is not instantly spent, then you'll have to have a treasurer or some one responsible for holding on to the money and paying expenses as they're incurred.

One group of women I heard from collected annual dues of $100.00 to pay for renting a meeting place, refreshments, and donating any dues money left at the end of each year to charity.

You may decide to collect monthly dues at each meeting or once a year. Dues for the BWLG are currently $25.00 a year.

What will dues cover?

Will dues cover operating expenses only, or operating expenses *and* refreshments? Some groups save excess dues to fund an annual party. Others, as noted above, have charitable agendas like the PALM Society in Hartford, which donates art to a local museum.

Will refreshments be served?

Refreshments served at book clubs go from tea, coffee and cheese and crackers to sit-down dinners. Groups that meet on the weekends can choose to go pot-luck, because members are usually coming directly from home, and it's more convenient.

When a host provides refreshments at her own expense, the simplicity or extravagance of the preparation will be as diverse and distinctive as members' finances and personalities. Perhaps to avoid members feeling that they can't compete with the lavish spread that another member provided, you may want to decide on an amount to spend on the meals.

If you're meeting in a book store or a library, the kinds of refreshments will be dictated by what is permitted at that particular location. Because the BWLG meets after work, I have all refreshments ready and available at six-thirty. Members coming directly from work are often ready to eat something by then. Some of our other members who aren't working, or who are able to eat before coming, may be ready for desert. One smaller group that I spoke with discussed books over a full course dinner at the dining room table. While another, meeting at the office, is happy to discuss books over a meal at the caferteria.

Inquire about food allergies, or other dietary restrictions so that you can avoid a potentially harmful ingredient in a recipe. Because many people today are eliminating red meat from their diet, these members should be considered when planning menus. Refreshment suggestions are at the end of Chapter 3.

Who provides refreshments?

If you rotate meetings at members homes, does the hostess provide all refreshments? Making this equitable takes a little thought. Some things to keep in mind are that members come and go. If there're more members than months, or if each member is not able to host, it's possible that members may leave the group before ever having a turn, and others may be asked to host more than once during the year. Will you decide to go pot-luck? Deciding on pot-luck can be more than you bargained for, especially when a main dish arrives late, or worse, doesn't arrive at all.

Another alternative is asking members to make a specified monetary donation at each meeting to cover costs. Since the BWLG always meets at my home, I consider them guests and provide all the refreshments. Though occasionally a members will bring a main dish, appetizer, or wine simply because they want to.

Are RSVPs required for each meeting?

Requiring members to RSVP is especially important if the hostess is providing all of the refreshments, or if you're renting space. You may not want to ask a book store to remain open just for your group if you don't have a quota, and especially if they're charging a fee. RSVPs are common courtesy. Decide how far in advance you need to receive the response.

What is the ideal size of a group?

This is a very important decision. Do you want to limit size? I stated earlier that a group can function with as few as three, though more people make for a more interesting group. Too many, and total chaos exists; no one is heard. Quality of thought is what increases the level of discussion.

What is the ideal number?

First, let me say that a large membership is not always indicative of how large your core group, those who regularly attend meetings, will be. Some groups have a membership of forty to fifty members, with twenty showing at any one meeting. Others limit membership, allowing a newcomer only when a member leaves.

My feeling is that a group should be a manageable number. Sitting in a circle...a circle of sisterhood...or a semblence of one, where everyone faces each other, is the ideal. There's something spiritual about circles; people tend to be more spontaneous in this setting. However, the circle must be close enough for everyone to be heard. Too large a group, and this isn't possible.

One of the problems with too large a group is that spontaneity is lost. Another is that members who tend to be timid are more timid in larger groups. Too often it isn't until the end of the meeting that members realize that a particular member wasn't heard. (In the Discussion section, I've written about a couple of activities that will encourage the reticent member's participation.)

When are new members allowed to join?

Allowing members to join anytime of the year puts the group in constant flux. On the other hand, welcoming members year round constantly adds interesting and new people to the group.

By limiting the number of members, the group becomes exclusive. Limiting membership gives you an opportunity to get to know your members better. It's your group, you decide who, and how many. Whatever works best work for you.

Literary Sisters, in Cambridge, Massachusetts, limits membership to fourteen, and new members are accepted by invitation only. The group allows members to take a leave of absence, and members with four absences are asked to leave the group.

The BWLG consists of nine of my best friends, and others with whom I'm affiliated through a mutual organization to which several of us belong, and then others whom I've met because of the group. New members are allowed to join anytime, and this works well for us. When BWLG was mentioned in an edition of *American Visions* magazine, I received a call from a woman who was eager to connect with Black women. Though she lived not too far from me, she didn't know that our book group existed. We welcomed her with open arms to our circle of Black women. She credits the group with saving her sanity. I'd hate to think of her having to wait a year to have joined us.

FWO—for women only!

This is a major decision. The dynamics of your group can be determined not only by gender but by the male/female ratio. Most women enjoy the opportunity to be among other women, this is probably the reason most book discussion groups are FWO (For Women Only). Not all women are able or want to belong to sororities or to other "women-only groups" with agendas pertinent to women. These groups are larger and can be impersonal.

However, FWO is not for everyone. One single member of the BWLG left because she prefered to spend her free time in a setting where there was a possibility of meeting someone of the opposite sex. A group that is FWO obviously doesn't have the benefit of a male perspective, and the dynamics of the group will be profoundly affected. "Girl talk," wherever it may lead, is an invaluable component to FWO groups however.

Not FWO!

There's no mystery to forming a coed book discussion group. Though most groups are FWO, many welcome both men and women. The Book Club in Boynton Beach, Florida, was established in 1992, and The Community Book Forum, in Baton Rouge, Louisiana, has been operating successfully since 1976.

Fifty percent of the twenty members of New York's Griot Society are men. The group was established in 1994, and founder Bonita Lockley says the founding committee decided it was important to include men "in order to have a balanced perspective about books they would read."

This was an important decision for the group, whose male members decidedly voted against reading fiction. According to Lockley it is the Griot Society's reading list, heavily weighted with history, biography, and poetry books, that prompted several of the male members to join.

Statistically speaking, most men tend to enjoy reading nonfiction, while women tend to read fiction. When deciding whether or not your group will include men, you'll have to consider the types of books the group will read. I've mentioned that the BWLG decided at our Interest Meeting that, despite the fact that many of the men in our lives read, we wanted a night out by ourselves, for ourselves; thus, the BWLG is FWO.

FMO or Mixers?

Though I didn't come across any, I've heard that a few discussion groups are FMO (For Men Only). I knew of one group where the predominant composition was couples; some were married, some were dating, and there were a few singles of both sexes. Most confessed that the reason the other had joined was not only because they wanted to read, but because the meetings presented an opportunity to be with their partners. I was also informed that over the years, two relationships developed because of the group. Meeting at a book discussion group you know you have something in common, and most definitely, something to talk about.

Most books I've read have at least one male character. If your group decides to concentrate on fiction, this would be a consideration when deciding to make your agenda for a mixed group. Some

• • • • • • • • • • • • • •

I've had the pleasure of meeting

extremely interesting women from all

walks of life and a variety of age

groups. I epecially like the comraderie

and the bonding I receive from all-

Black female reading groups.

—*Shari Hubert*

• • • • • • • • • • • • • •

groups invite men in only for a particular book. The presence of men and input from them have the potential to be especially inter-esting and provocative.

Mother-daughter

The Mother-Daughter Book Club, located in Washington, D.C., was founded by Shireen Dodson for mothers and their daughters. Their current membership consists of twelve moms and thirteen daughters, ranging in age from eight to eleven, who meet once a month on Sunday afternoons. Mother and daughter(s) co-host dis-cussions. One mom, Linda Chastang says this gives mothers "an opportunity to know what our daughters are reading, how they are thinking, and to help them refine their analytical skills." The moth-ers obtain a book list, make a selection of three books from which their daughters select the one to read at the meetings. Discussions facilitated and hosted by a mother-daughter team help to develop invaluable leadership skills for the young women.

Peer Specific?

Do you want to limit membership to only teachers, suburbanites, over thirty, sorors, frat brothers, etc.? If this is your pleasure, it's perfectly alright. While you may have reasons for wanting to make yours an exclusive group, having an inclusive group has its benefits. It's a way to broaden your circle of friends and sphere of influence.

Ethnic/multi-ethnic?

Because ethnic women often have fewer opportunities to meet with other ethnic women for bonding and, as did our literary sisters generations ago, for intellectual-stimulation, this is an important issue. On the other hand, having a group comprised of many ethnicities opens the group up to other perspectives. Books that a homogenous group would read are not necessarily those that a multi-ethnic group would read, so there's the opportunity to be introduced to new reading experiences.

People of a certain age?

On the plus side, older members offer yet another point of view that can provide a wonderful opportunity to gain insight. At one time, the oldest member in the BWLG was seventy-two, and the two youngest were twenty, one of them being the seventy-two year old's granddaughter.

On the negative side, some members may not feel comfortable discussing or facilitating a book like *Black Erotica*, edited by Miriam DeCosta Willis. Often younger members feel inhibited in the presence of someone old enough to be their mother or grandmother, or, conversely, older members may feel uncomfortable with someone young enough to be their young daughter. This is just another thing to be considered.

Are guests welcomed?

Will you permit guests by invitation only, or not at all? Literary

Sisters, in Cambridge, has designated the month of April to welcome guests. You may decide to allow guests to come unannounced to any meeting.

Obviously, "by invitation only" makes for stability within the group. A new person popping in *whenever* can be disruptive, because introductions seem to be never ending. That feeling of "family," the reason some members to want to join the group in the first place, may become elusive.

Members who want to bring guest should ask in advance. After all, a facilitator who has prepared a special activity for a particular book may be inhibited when displaying real feelings regarding sensitive issues (i.e., regarding relationships with men, sex, race, religion) in front of strangers, especially if that stranger is male, of another race, religion. etc. Groups dynamics will, after just a few get-togethers, establish themselves, with members quickly feeling comfortable with one another.

Perhaps you may want to decide that guests are permitted only twice a year, an exception being if someone is entertaining a house guest and, rather than not attend a meeting, is allowed to bring the guest. In this case the host and the facilitator should be informed in advance.

Children? Should members be allowed to bring their children?
Whether children are allowed to come will first depend on the location of the meeting, and how old the children are. One of the most devoted members of the BWLG is a single mom and couldn't afford to come if she had to get a babysitter for her seven-year old daughter. So she brings her daughter along. The daughter is well-behaved and goes downstairs to the den, where she does her homework or watches television or dozes while we're upstairs. Members are not even aware until they leave that she's there at all. However, if she were the kind who needed her mother's attention every five minutes, or if she were too young to be downstairs on her own, we'd have to give this situation serious consideration.

It is best to set up operational guidelines prior to the group's first meeting. If you set guidelines in the beginning that are given to each member when they join, your group will run more smoothly. In the case of children, if you do not want children at the meeting, then you should discretely ask potential candidates about their situation. The policy on children should definitely be agreed upon at the Interest Meeting not when you're hit in the face with the decision. You want all members to be clear on this.

The following is an example of a possible scenerio: Your best friend wants to bring your new godchild, an adorable four-month old, or perhaps her rambunctious two-year-old grandchild. You panic. No one enjoys a child, no matter how adorable, who is squealing while you're trying to watch a movie you paid for. The meeting situation is no different from going to a movie. The child's presence will definitely be a constant disturbance to members who, mind you, came to discuss books.

If founding members make a decision on children, and if this decision is clearly stated in the organizational manual, then there should be no hurt feelings when you have to say no.

Officers

Having officers gives the membership a sense of formality and officialdom to the group. By assigning officers such as president, secretary, public relations, treasurer, you are giving your elected members responsibility, and that's a reflection of not only how serious the group is, but also how seriously members take their involvement with the group. Even so, many groups function quite well with one person doing everything that needs to be done until an event necessitates a position be established or the delegation of authority, however brief.

Naming the group

At the Interest Meeting ask the group to think about an appropriate name for the discussion group. While the name can be decided on later, discussion on this topic is a good way to commit them to the group.

Some groups select straight-forward names such as Brothers & Sisters, The Book Club, or Bunch for Lunch. However, others are creative, choosing names such as, Imani Nia (Faith), or S.I.L.K. (Sisters in Literary Kaleidoscopes). Still others have no name. I met one woman who'd been in a discussion group for eighteen years that she fondly referred to as "my book group," or "my reading group." This proves that it's people who make the group, not the name.

What kinds of books will to read?

Do you want to read just one type of book, e.g. mysteries, biographies, fiction, or do you want to read everything?

Once you've assessed what the group appetite is for, I would suggest that you gently nudge them to try other, related kinds of books. For instance, if the group is only interested in reading women authors, suggest for the group's fifth novel a male novelist who writes through the eyes of a female, like Ernest Gaines' *Autobiography of Miss Jane Pittman*. If they are only interested in romance novels, suggest for the fifth novel one of Walter Mosely's Easy Rollins adventures or one of Chester Himes marvelous detective tales.

Will you read only contemporary books? Are you going to try to locate some written during the first or second World Wars, and earlier? More and more of the books written in the thirties and earlier are being republished. Along those same lines, will you read short stories, poetry, autobiographies, or only novels? Each have their own merit, and the choice is either an individual or group decision. Your group may decide to allow each facilitator to decide on the book; what the group will read for the discussion she or he will facilitate.

If you decide to read a collection of short stories, one approach to discussion may be to assign two stories to a one or two members who would do the research, make a report, and plan an activity around the story/stories they've read. The life of the group as a reading group does depend on its having a sense of reading as a kind of adventure. An open mind is key to any successful reading group.

As to genres, I think it is very important that the group keep an open mind. (See Chap. 2 for more detailed information about books.)

Which books to read...who decides?

Will members in succession decide? Or will a committee or the entire group? Depending on the size of the group, I think it is best to have the group decide what it wants to read. Each member voting is a much more democratic process, one that assures each member that she has input in what's going on.

If, for example, the theme for the February reading is Caribbean literature, and there is within the group someone versed in that kind of work, it's probably a good idea to allow a special selection. Whatever you decide here, the group can always change its mind. I've always felt that it is important to experiment. As the group solidifies, find what is best for you and your members.

Paperback or hardcover?

Will you read only the less-expensive paperbacks, knowing that you must wait at least a year for newly released books to appear in in book stores? Since this only affects newly published books, it won't be too much of a problem. However, if you're truly a book lover, you won't think about the cost and will prefer the hardcover book because it holds up better over time. This is especially important if you're interested in establishing a library or in collecting. As long as the work in question isn't an abridged (shortened) version, the hardcover vs. paperback controversey is not an issue, but a matter of choice, or economics.

Obtaining books

Will one member order and pick up books for the group? Ask your local book dealers store if they'll be willing to offer a book club discount. Check with publishers (ask for the Sales and Marketing Dept.) to ascertain if they'll give the club a discount. Any arrangement that works for your group is good.

Will the group have a newsletter?

Though not absolutely necessary, a newsletter is one way to communicate with and keep up with the group. The newsletter published by You Go Girls includes a letter from the editor and co-founder Jean Weathers, called "You Go Girl of the Month"—spotlighting a member each month, and offering minutes of last meeting, a Critic's Corner, a review of books, and a calendar of upcoming events, to mention a few of the items contained within their six-page periodical. Newsletters are also great ways to maintain an historical record of the group. Ms. C. from Literary Sisters gave me copies of four years of newsletters. These were wonderful for getting a feel for the history of the group. Whether this comes under the P.R. person's responsibility or the secretary's will be another one of the decisions to be made.

If you decide to start a newsletter, the expense of the newsletter should be covered by dues. A decision would have to be made as to who will be responsible for typing, printing, and deciminating the newsletter.

Before the meeting ends, be sure to:

- decide on a book for the first official meeting.

- identify a facilitator—the one who'll lead the discussion—for the next meeting. (The responsibilities of the facilitator are in Chap. 3)
- Collect everyone's address and contact information. You then list and publish this information in a handout consisting of

rules, bylaws, etc. decided upon in this Interest Meeting, mailing this information to each member before the first official meeting or distibuting it at that meeting.

So, your intoductory book discussion group meeting is over, and you're ready to begin!

However before the first meeting, you, in your capacity as group organizer, should type up the guidelines that were decided on at the Interest Meeting, and mail them to each member, requesting that comments be sent prior to meeting. Literary Sisters suggests that at the first meeting you should briefly go over the club rules and give each member a notebook containing:

- Club rules, dues, and guidelines

- Names and addresses of members

- Directions to member's homes. (Members should bring enough copies of directions to their home to pass out to each member.)

- Hostess list

- Book notices and reviews

- Upcoming reading list

- Facilitators (discussion leaders)

- Book sources

Notebooks or folders should have pockets to hold handouts. *Now you're ready to begin the discussion.*

Chapter 2

SELECTING BOOKS
FOR DISCUSSION

• • • • • • • • • • • • • •

Our discussion allows

us to tap into deep

personal feelings and

occasionally bring to the

surface some forgotten

memory that shows us

who we really are.

—Carole Alkins

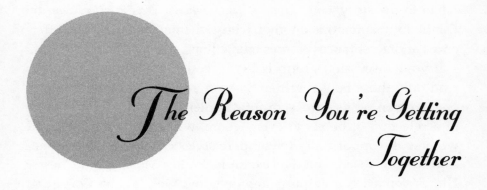

The Reason You're Getting Together

If you've decided to read only books written by one particular ethnic group, life style, race, or gender, you should ask yourself under what circumstances will the group vary?

For example: If your membership is all-Black, will you discuss a book written by a non-Black? If yes, under what circumstances? The Black Women's Literary Guild, though committed to reading only those books written by Black authors, did read *A Feast of All Saints*, by Anne Rice. The book came *highly* recommended by a group member who said that it was about the mulatto community in New Orleans, that it was unbelievably real, and that Rice wrote with authenticity about her subject. Most of those discussing the book enjoyed the story and did not see a problem over the fact that Rice is White. However, we have not read any other fiction by a non-Black writer. Because I've heard from so many groups from across the country, who are all raving about *Along Came a Spider* (a book by James Patterson, another non-Black), this thriller with

Black characters will probably end up on the BWLG's book list. The theme of *The Joy Luck Club* by Amy Tan, about Chinese-American mother-daughter relationships, is so universal that any group can relate to the story. *Once Upon a Time When I Was Puerto Rican* by Esmeralda Santiago is another whose theme about cultural differences and acceptances crosses ethnic lines.

If your discussion group is FWO, you can make a decision to read only those books written by women without offending anyone. Women writers are as prolific as men. Now that there is more of a selection of books in every genre, written by both men and women, the opportunity to compare styles can add a new dimension to your discussion. For example, Walter Mosley and Chester Himes' female counterparts are alive and well; Lucha Corpi and Eleanor Taylor Bland write wonderful detective novels. Tananarive Due wrote an absolutely thrilling surrealist book entitled, *The Between*. Still, I would suggest the group keep an open mind.

. . . .

I joined the reading club in order to have

someone to discuss books with, and I look

forward to, and attend, the discussion

even if I haven't read the book

—*Pearl Owens*

. . . .

Selecting the First Book

Selecting the first book is important! It's like making a good first impression, so select carefully. You may lose those members who aren't yet fully committed to the concept of reading a book selected by someone else and having to have it completed within a relatively short time frame.

Of course, you can always check the best-seller lists. However, if you're looking for books of a particular ethnicity your selection will be limited. Subscribing to magazines and journals, obtaining copies of them from your local book store, or enrolling in one of the ethnically focused mail order book clubs will at least make you aware of the many books being published. For a description of some of these publications and others, see Appendices: Book Sources.

Of course, you can always wait to hear about a good book through "The Girlfriends' Network," but then what's "good" is subjective, i.e., subject to those books that girlfriend enjoyed or didn't, and you know we don't all like the same thing. *The*

Serpent's Gift by Helen Elaine Lee was a "Didn't like" by most members in one group, while another reported that it was the only book that the entire group had enjoyed.

While the BWLG, in Massachusetts, loved *The Wedding* by Dorothy West; the You Go Girl, in Illinois, liked it least.

Unless there's a "hot" best seller out, a suggestion for a first book (particularly for Blacks who want to read Black women writers) with which you can't go wrong is *Their Eyes Were Watching God* by Zora Neale Hurston. This book is now considered a masterpiece, and read in more schools and colleges than any other book written by a Black author. "What was Janie searching for?" You can ask what each of the men in Janie's life were looking for when they married her. "What is the symbolism of the horizon?"

Another that I'd suggest as a first book, if no one can think of anything, is *Long Distance Life* by Marita Golden. It's a multigenerational story that deals with relationships, contemporary social problems, and love of family. The facilitator of this book needed to ask only one question and the group kept the discussion going for the rest of the evening. That magic question was: "To what do you think the long distance life in the title referred? Was it the actual number of years covered in the book, and the lives involved, or was it the spiritual distance between the mother and daughter, mother and son, father and son?"

As readers you know that books can vicariously take you around the world. As an added dimension to the meetings, you may want to pinpoint the locales of each book you read on a map. For example, *Middle Passage* by Charles Johnson, takes you to New Orleans; *Waiting to Exhale* by Terry McMillan, to Arizona; *Tree of Life* by Maryse Condé, to the Caribbean; *The Devil's Hatband* by Robert Greer, to Colorado; *Soul to Soul* by Yelena Khanga, to Russia; and *Like Water for Chocolate* by Laura Esquivel to Mexico. Discussions can be enhanced by providing the group with information about the locale.

This vicarious "journey" can extend to refreshments (see pp. XX). At some point the group may decide to take a trip to one of the places about which member's have read, or eat foods representative of a particular location. Literary Sojourners, an offshoot of the BWLG, journeyed to Hartford, Connecticut, to see a wonderful stage production of *Bailey's Cafe* by Gloria Naylor. After which, we were plesantly surprised when Naylor led a Question and Answer session.

Always remember that:

- Best sellers are not always the best choices for discussion, so don't decide to select a book just because its on the best seller list.

- Each book selection will not appeal to every member. Respect and honor the decision of whomever recommends the book. You might get a few members saying, I absolutely hate science fiction. Then when it has to be read for group discussion, some of these former nay-sayers will even become the best discussants for the evening. Occasionally, this exposure and the subsequent discussion, in particular, makes one a convert.

- By mixing up selections you're bound in the course of the year to make each member happy. Though most of the members in the BWLG moan when a self-help book such as *In the Company of My Sisters*, by Julia Boyd, or *Tapping the Power Within* by Iyanla Vanzant, is suggested, these books make for excellent discussion. I'd suggest that at least once a year a self-help book be read as a way to allow members to share experiences and talk about related incidents. These meetings always turn out to be a catharsis that has everyone exclaiming what a great meeting it was.

- Books that weren't particularly enjoyable often lead to the most stimulating discussion. Some of the best discussions I've been a part of have been of those books that no one liked. It's not unusual for a member not to like a book, and then change her opinion once the book has been dissected and explained from various viewpoints during the discussion. Gwen, a member of the BWLG, shared her feelings after reading Mosley's *White Butterfly*: "When I came to the meeting, I really didn't care to read another book by Mosley, but after the discussion, I might."

- The value of being a part of a discussion group is best demonstrated when everyone respects opposing views and different interpretations. If the sum of our experiences makes us unique, then expect and graciously accept different interpretations. During the discussion of *Migrations of the Heart* by Marita Golden, Shari remarked: "I really enjoyed the book and the writing style of Marita Golden. " Gert also had positive feelings about the book, saying: "Marita went to Nigeria to follow her heart, but she ended up migrating back to her roots to find her real self." On the other hand, Marva commented: "Marita didn't connect the themes she began with to the ending. I was disappointed that she didn't give us more insight about family, community, and love across generations. I did relive my own experiences in Nigeria as I read the wonderful descriptions of the country. But I wanted more."

When we read Nathan McCall's *Makes Me Wanna Holler*, Bettye, a writer, emphatically announced that she "did not like the book!" and that her young adult daughter Nicole said that the book sounded as though it were written by a twelve-year-old girl. Bettye was "happy to learn that the book was self-published, and not exploited by a White publisher." On the other hand, Karen and Vickie "loved the book!"

- Deciding when to assign a particular book can be tricky. Books not known as "light reading," e.g., *Parable of the Sower*, by science fiction writer Octavia Butler, should not be assigned in the summer, or during the holidays when the concentration level is lowest. During these times, something you can finish in an evening or two, read at the beach or on a noisey train is a better suggestion.

Reading and Preparing a Book for Discussion

People read for different reasons. Some read for pure enjoyment, to be entertained. They want nothing heavy, nothing they have to think about. Others prefer the heavy stuff: themes that they have to think about or that might provoke them to action.

One reader will say she didn't like the writer's style. Didn't like the story or didn't like a particular character. Or that the character's development was incomplete. Another will feel that the story was poorly written or had too much sex. Still, another reader will see the book completly differently.

Reading a book in preparation for a formal discussion group is different from reading for pure enjoyment.

When reading for enjoyment, it's okay if, after completing the book, you don't remember names, dates, and places. When reading for discussion it is *not* okay. Imagine what would happen at a discussion group if no one remembered anything!

First, you need to read with more concentration, paying close attention to detail—although not with so much attention that you aren't enjoying the book. You want to keep in mind what the author is trying to say. You have to think about the book and try to get more deeply inside the character than you would if you were reading for pleasure. Those little stickey notes are great for "flagging" pages to which you, as the discussant, want to refer during the meeting either because:

1. You want clarification on something;

2. You want to quickly recall a point;

3. You want to remember the character's name and their relationship to the story.

Chapter 3

THE FIRST MEETING

· · · · · · · · · · · · · · ·

The group is an opportu-

nity to discuss what I've

read with women I admire

who, while sharing similar

values, bring different and

interesting perspectives to

the discussion and to my

connection with the book.

— *Marva Nathan*

Facilitating—
Leading a Discussion

Every discussion group needs a facilitator. A facilitator is someone who leads the discussion, is prepared to pick up the slack in the conversation, and can keep the group focused. The facilitator's role can be a wonderful learning, skill-enhancing experience, it can also be challenging.

The good faciliator, like a talk show host, knows when to interrupt a long-winded member, as well as to urge a quiet member to go further. Some groups limit the number of minutes a member can talk by using a "talking stick". The "talking stick", which can be an actual stick or designated object, is passed to the person wanting to talk. As long as the speaker is holding the stick, the rest of the group gives the speaker the respect of listening. I think that the spontaneity adds to the excitement of the discussion. Personally, I've never experienced a discussant who talked too long, but my group consists of many dynamic individuals. Our jump-in-there format works for us, reducing the role of the facilitator. I'm not advocating it for every group.

The facilitator also has to be alert to one who is digressing and/or straying irrelevantly from the book and has to be able to tactfully get them back on track. As facilitator, you may even have to stop someone who interrupts the speaker, at least long enough for the speaker's point to be made. One of the facilitator's most important jobs, though, is to listen.

When discussing Wallace Thurman's *The Blacker the Berry*, one facilitator researched the time period (i.e., the 1930's) and handed out a fact sheet that helped the group get a reference relating to the story line. It helped the group to understand why the protagonist and other characters thought the way they did.

When the BWLG discussed Dorothy West's *The Wedding*, we invited another group to join us, and actually held a "wedding reception" that included a bride, with a white gown, mother of the bride, attendants, a two-tier cake. We handed out programs, and yes, even threw rice. We thought of everything imaginable, except the groom. Because most of our members have been to Martha's Vineyard, the book's locale had a lot of meaning, and we shared many personal stories relating to experiences on the island. While most of us enjoyed the overall story, we all agreed that the end was not as well written as the beginning, unlike many of Ms. West's other stories.. Her first novel, *The Living Is Easy*, a more immediate, more finely crafted work, written in 1948, was unanimously voted the better, by far, of the two books. I'd like to see *The Living Is Easy* mandatory reading in every American history class, social studies class, English lit class, and most definitely every African American studies class. It very aptly covers each of these disciplines in a remarkable way.

Another group reported that after reading Ilayna Vanzant's, *The Value in the Valley*, an inspirational book about overcoming obstacles in life, the facilitator gave each member five smooth stones; symbolic of the stones with which David slew Goliath. The group was instructed to place the stones on a piece of Kente cloth as a way of connecting with our roots and to rub the stones whenever they had a problem.

When the BWLG read *When and Where I Enter* by Paula Giddens, after giving a brief synopsis of the book, the facilitator asked each discussant to share when and where she felt she had "entered" (became her own person). After a moment of silence while everyone processed the request, one after another members shared thoughts relating when they felt they became the woman they wanted to be. One member, then seventy-two, shared that she'd "entered" when at fifty-two she walked out on her alcoholic husband, got a job, developed interests, purchased a home. She was proud that she had been able to prove to herself she could do it. Another shared how at about forty-five she'd had a heart-to-heart talk with her mother about something that had been festering with her mother for about twenty-five years; afterwhich the air was cleared, and her mother was able to put the past behind her and go forward. One fifty- year-old artist, who was a nearing the end of a self-imposed decision to be a stay-at-home mom, admitted that she didn't think she'd entered yet. The group was physically spent when the discussion was over, but we unanimously decided that it was the best discussion we'd ever had.

There are so many ways to begin. When discussing *Ugly Ways*, by Tina McElroy, the facilitator asked each member to use the words beginning with the letters in the book's title to describe the mother's character and explain why they thought those words were apt. *Ugly Ways* was a book that was described by a member of group from California as "one of those bad mama books." Mu'dear—— a term of endearment for mother dear, commonly found in the South——was not your typical loving mom. Words from the title that may best describe "Mu'dear" could be: "Unusual"...Mu'dear, as stated above, was not your typical mom. "Gardener"...Mu'dear slept and bathed herself in lavender bath salts during the day, and as strange as it seems, gardened at night. "Love"...was the family's last name, however, a lengthy discussion could take place about whether or not the family members actually had love for one another, or even themselves.

This format of directing a question directly to members is an important strategy for soliciting comments from members who, though they never miss a meeting, are passive participants.

A Book Under Discussion

Give a little background of author: Helen Elaine Lee, author of The Serpent's Gift, *a first novel, is a graduate of Harvard College and Harvard law school. Her father is a lawyer, her mother a professor. Helen Elaine comes from a storytelling family and drew upon a few of her family members for the characters in the book. She says that LaRue is much like her grandfather, and that the lesbian lovers were modeled after her favorite aunt who had a female lover.*

Give an overview of the book: The Serpent's Gift *is about the endurance of Black families, two midwestern families in particular, the Smalls and the Staples; the importance of self-love, the day-to-day struggles of marriage, and the liberating power of overcoming the painful past. The novel begins in 1910, spaning over sixty years to the 1970s—though you learn something of the period going back to the years just after the Civil War.*

Give an accessment of the author's credibility: Coming from a storytelling family, the author was knowlegable about the African tradition of storytelling, where the highly respected griot (storyteller) would gather the village people and would, much like a minister, tell stories that had a moral —how the world began, how minding other people's business will get you in trouble—basically stories that told people how they should live their lives.

Suggested Opening Questions for the Facilitator

- Often authors give clues to the book in the title, or in the names of the characters. Knowing the title, and before reading the book, what did you think the book would be about?

- What about the names of the two families in *The Serpent's Gift*? How were their surnames—Ruby and Polaris Staples, Eula and Ontario Smalls—a foreshadowing of the character of the two families.

- The book opens with Vesta's 71st birthday, and she is pouring brandy into a hand-cut crystal glass that she uses because she thinks it adds dignity to her tattered dresser scarf and plastic covered couch. She says, "She never had a drink without a reason, and she drank only the best." By the end of the book, knowing what we do about Vesta, is this characteristic of her?

- What is the symbolism or the meaning of Ontario's "cancelling time with the swallowing of each cloth covered button?"

- When Ontario falls, Lee writes that "the spectators followed him to earth, with their heads moving down in unison?" What is the captivation that people have with tragic events, whether watching a fire or egging someone on who is contemplating a suicidal jump?

- We know that Ontario was an abuser and drank quite a bit. We also know that Vesta was dark-skinned. Do you think Ontario believed that Vesta wasn't his child?

- The truth about Ontario's death was kept from LaRue for many years. Vesta's character was shaped in part because she'd witnessed her father's abusive ways. LaRue was a happy-go-lucky-type. He loved Olive and his child, and was basically a decent person. How do you think his character would have been affected had he known the truth about his father earlier? Pg 94*

- How do you interpret Vesta's dream that "Ontario had wings that grew fleshy from his work clothed shoulder blades and saved him from his fall as they unfolded, easing him to the ground?"

- What was the significance of Vesta's making samplers, with the border of each getting wider and wider with each succeeding sampler?

- What was the significance, if any with Vesta's obsession with white colored clothes? At what point in her life did this obsession come about? pg 105

- After LaRue's story about the brussel sprouts, why did Zella think that Vesta was hurt by the story? pg. 108

- Why do you think LaRue was left to tell Ruby's story? pg 109

- LaRue says that he "had to remember in order to let go." And "You have to go away before you can come back." What did he mean by those statements? pg 113

- Any loving parent protects and defends his or her child at all costs. Can you explain why Ruby's father chose not to defend his child? pg 158

* Page numbers

- Why did Ouida play a "cat and mouse" game with Flood? pg 179

- I loved LaRue's story about gaining hope, strength and courage. What did you think about it? Why? p218

- Zella loved Ouida, and Ouida says, "It was Zella that she'd chosen and Zella that she loved." Was she being truthful? Afterall, Ouida only "settled" for Zella after becoming too ill to care for herself. p238

- Why did LaRue decide not to recane the rocking chair, leaving it with a hole? p268

- What was the humming sound referred to as "a sound like lightening wires plucked now and then?"

- If Zella loved Ouida, and wasn't ashamed of her relationship, why didn't she kiss Ouida in front of Emeritus? p328

- What was Ouida's premonition of light? p335

- What did LaRue mean when he called Emeritus a "hood ornament? p336

- Of all the females in the book, the only one who had a strong character was Ruby, and she died early. Did this concern you? Why?

- Vesta, though absolutely devoted to Desi, never said she loved her but that she "owned" her. Which two characters would you say showed the most love for the other? Why?

- At least three autumn colors are mentioned in the book. What are they?

- The title of the book is *The Serpent's Gift*. Which character was most serpent-like in shedding and renewing his or her life?

- How different would things have been had Ruby lived?

- Do you think Ouida fell in love with Zella because she was in search of a mother figure?

- In the beginning of the book, Vesta, with her eyes closed, is laying on the sofa holding an orange. She says, "It feels like the color orange." Do you think colors emit a sensation that allows someone to tell what color it is? Explain.

- Who was your favorite character? Why?

- What do you think about Helen Elaine Lee's writing? I thought she was quite lyrical, reminding me of James Baldwin: "She inhaled the dark, dark smell of the coffee, as it dripped, and touched the beaded mist collecting at the rim of her cup with her fingertips."

- Do you think the author to be a feminist? Explain.

- Would you read another book by this author?

The Facilitator might conclude with: I think the message the author is conveying is that family is the lifeline for African Americans, and that the people who succeed are those who remain open to life and love. Those who are able to move through life letting go (shedding) negative influences (pains of slavery) and moving on. *The Serpent's Gift* is life and death and the gift of renewal.

The book we read before Lee's, *R.L's Dream* by Walter Mosley, talked in part about the extended family and dreams also. Coincidently, the book we read right after, *The Value in the Valley* by Iyanla Vanzant, continues the theme of survival; going on.

A Book Discussion in Action

In 1992, at the height of the *Waiting to Exhale* frenzy, the Black Women's Literary Guild broadcast a book discussion on a local cable network.

That evening, the group discussion facilitator was Marva, a forty-something divorced mother of three adult children, two boys, and a girl. The discussants were Martha, a married, forty something mother of two, a boy and a girl; Pat, over fifty, married for twenty-five years to the man she'd dated for ten, and a mother of adult children, a boy and girl; Fran, in her late thirties, married and with a young son; Barbara, in her late forties, married for twenty years, and the mother of a boy approaching adulthood, and a girl aged fifteen; Gaye, our only unmarried, never-been-married, who'd like a committed relationship; and Kate, a single mom who, in her mid-forties, has two adult sons, and a five-year old daughter. None of these women look their ages, they're all professionals, active and involved outside of the home, and none can really relate to the women in

Waiting to Exhale, especially Pat who began dating her husband when she was eighteen, and still considers him her best friend.

The following dialogue, taken in part from a transcript of the video, will give you an idea of how a discussion should flow. Please note Marva's comments. She is an example of the quintessential facilitator. She set the group up, played devil's advocate, tossed out leading questions, and steered the group in one direction or another while being careful never to dominate the discussion. [Author's note: This is a book that should have been discussed twice. Once with women only, so you could yell and holler, and "Oh, girl," 'til your hearts content. And another where you invite men to get their perspective.]

M: Tonight we're going to discuss Waiting to Exhale. *This book has opened up some important dialogue between men and women and among Black women everywhere. Does anyone have an opening comment they'd like to share?*

K: Friendship is what stood out the most for me, the friendship they all seemed to portray, even though they went through many trials and tribulations. And though they didn't always agree, they were willing to accept where they were, and why they were there, unconditionally.

G: I think one unifying thing was that they were in the same place although their ages varied. They all shared one thing, their interest in finding a male partner.

M: I noticed that two of the people in the book, Savannah and Robin, were told in the first person, while Bernadine and Gloria were in the third person. I wonder if that had any significance?

Mt: Terry McMillan said that of all the women in the book,

Savannah is most like her, not her, but most like her. So maybe that's the reason she was able to give her a voice.

F: I saw Savannah as having a relationship with her mother, while Robin was attached to her father. What was Savannah looking for? Why was she constantly moving? Searching for herself—and a man.

K: My first impression was not that she was so much searching for herslf, but that she was ambitious. Striving, achieving. A successful person...Her moves to other cities were for professional success, and until she met Robin, men weren't paramount.

M: *I think one of the things that Terry McMillan does is to help us look at female sexuality and what female sexuality means to Black women.*

P: Are these typical females? They seem to have over-zealous sexual appeties. What I mean is that the story's one you usually read about men, not one you read about women. This is a book in which not one, but all four women were Black and professional. All four were also looking for a man and weren't ashamed of the fact.

K: I think it's an age thing. We're of a different age from these women, so we think differently. How old are they, 27 to 40? We're kind of over the hill, societally thinking, and don't think the same way.

Mt: I don't know what the dating scene is for 27 year olds now. Is that what happens? Like the scene in the bar. I've seen women out who are hoping that a man will pay attention to them as a sexual thing, while men don't seem to be quite as interested. Robin seemed more out there on the spectrum and didn't want to apologize for her sexual appetite.

P: If a man were doing what these women did, he wouldn't be called promiscuous.

F: Didn't one of Robin's friends say that she could find a relationship if she took the time? I think a lot of Robin's problem was self-inflicted. She was a very attractive woman who was attractive to men. Gloria, on the other hand, was just the opposite. She was not as attractive and didn't have an opportunity to date like Robin.

P: Did Gloria want dates? She was devoted to her son—don't you think she was content with this love?

F: She would have cherished a relationship with a man, though she had a strong, bonded relationship with her son and was a devoted mother. She went off her rocker when she found out her ex-husband was gay. So, she would have liked a sexual relationship, a partner.

Mt: She sort of hid behind her devotion to her son and her career.

K: That's where tradition comes in.

M: Let's talk about the other married woman, Bernadine. When the book opens she's married to John, and they're beginning to have difficulties. They have two small children. As the book progresses, John leaves, and she stays in the house. By the end of the book, she's had two other brief relationships, one with Herbert and one with James. How is she like Gloria?

Mt: In the beginning she's like Gloria in that she has sacrificed her dreams for her family. She helped John start the business and put what she wanted to do on hold.

M: *What was her dream?*

All: To be a caterer.

M: *Yes, that's something a lot of women do —feed them and smile, and feed them and smile, and. . .*

P: Can you really say that she put her dreams on hold, or was she controlled by a husband who wouldn't allow her to work?

M: *They were a very wealthy. He made $400,000 a year...*

F: He's in the computer business.

K: There was a sense of control. Here was a man with a need to control, so he kept her out of his business. That allowed him do the things he did, making her dependent.

P: Right, whenever you consider what eventually happened, she should have been more prepared. Let's face it, she was naive.

M: *He definitely was controlling.*

K: You saw that more during and after the divorce. He had everything in his mother's name, and in his partner's name. All she knew about was his $400,000 income. He removed her from his business, from himself, from his financial situation.

F: Something else, here was a successful Black business man

whose wife wouldn't have fulfilled the traditional image if she worked outside the home.

P: Many Black men consider it a sign of their success if their wives don't have a job, even if it is a career. Bernadine had helped her husband build his business so he knew that she was very capable.

K: I was thinking that what John did was non-traditional.

All: That's very traditional!

M: *Let's deal with that directly, let's take that head on. Who did John leave Bernadine for?*

All: His White secretary!

P: A twenty-five year old White secretary!

K: And he's forty. He wanted his Black wife to be tradition-al, to stay home, to be involved in the community, and to raise the children. However, when he left her he chose a White career woman.

M: *I suppose we could take another hour or two to discuss Black men who, upon gaining a level of success, leave their Black women behind for White women who ride the coat tails of success with them. But, time won't permit since there's so much to talk about the main characters.*

F: I thought Bernadine was a tremendous woman. Very strong, even though she came across as a weakling in the beginning.

K: I didn't see her as a weakling. I saw her fighting from the jump. Especially when she had the garage sale. To me, she took control of her life when she took his clothes, put them in his BMW, which he loved, threw gasoline on them, and burned them all!

Mt: And sold everything else, even the antique car at a garage sale for $1.00.

M: *Let's look at this more closely and its social significance. These are four Black women who are very strong, and I agree with you. I think she's a very strong woman who selectively dropped the ball, and we do that. We can be martyrs when we want, and we can be controlled when we want, and I think that's what happened to Bernadine.*

Mt: I think Black women tend to be stronger for other people than for themselves. Black women tend to champion other people and their causes rather than their own. I think that was one of the strengths McMillian gave these women, to ultimately be able to be strong for themselves.

K: Those are survival skills, and I think we Black women have them.

G: I agree that survival skills are innate, but I think we Black women get a lot more opportunities to practice them than some others.

M: *Some of what we do is because we've seen women who've gone before us do it that way. At least three of these women have mothers who are alive and active. Now I'd like us to think about where these women come from. What are the generations of women that came before them, and what's contributed to making them the women they are now? We started talking about Robin's parents, and Bernadine's. Robin has both parents. What did the generation before contribute to the person that is Robin?*

Robin's mother had a mastectomy, yet she was willing to sacrifice her health to care for her husband. But I think the doctor told her to go through a grieving process because the disease was going to get progressively worse. He was very brutal and hostile to her. There was a level of negativism from him that she endured, but inspite of her pain, she was devoted to her husband.

Mt: She had a relationship with Russell—she was always self-sacrificing. That was like her parent's in many respects. In other words, she was emulating exactly what her mother always did.

K: When you asked what role their parents played in their lives to me, Robin had a lot of expectations placed on her, and her character couldn't fulfill those expectations. Her sex life gave her that out—a level of freedom to make the decisions. She accepted herself. She did what she thought she had to do to make those decisions, to do it even if the gratification was instant and shortlived. Part of that is youth again. Young people don't live for tomorrow; they live for today, now. They don't see consequences. Only right now!

M: Robin was successful career-wise, however, she didn't feel she was getting her due.

Mt: She was always looking outside herself for things. She'd had her breasts augmented and was thinking about more cosmetic surgery.

K: Wasn't this indicative of her childhood? Her parents gave her everything. She never had to look within herself, and she wanted to be there for her parents in ways that were not possible.

Mt: One thing I noticed she didn't seem to respond to what her friends advised her. She kept thinking she should do something else. She overdressed. Wore too much makeup.

B: Didn't her friends tell her she was a 6 on a scale of 10— her friends telling her she didn't have to go to extremes?

M: *Robin is obsessive and compulsive in a lot of ways. Her relationships are bad relationships. She can't say no when she should. She shops when she's nervous. She shops when things go wrong. Has to have sex! Even if it's bad sex. Just has to have somebody there. Kate, I think you mentioned the value of solitude as opposed to loneliness.*

B: I wonder why she was like that when she had both parents.

P: Most of us don't have mortality staring us in the face. Robin did. She wasn't going to waste time. We don't know her as a teenager.

K: Somewhere in the book it talks about her seeing her father's illness progress. His illness did have an affect on her.

M: *I want to emphasize that these are smart women. These are people who lead successful lives, know how to get from college to a job. So what we're talking about is really just one facet of their lives. But it's a dominant facet because it hasn't really been explored in literature. These characters, as we look at them, are committed to family,*

to their work, their loves, and to themselves on some level. What real-
ly stands out for me so much is that they drop the ball when it comes
to taking charge of their personal relationships. Why do we keep giv-
ing to others and never nurturing ourselves? What is it that we are
afraid of, or that we ignore or deny?

Mt: I think we're socialized to do that as women, particularly as Black women. We're always looking to see that everyone
is taken care of. Men just look out for themselves. A woman
who appears to be self-sufficient is perceived negatively.
Because society has placed women in the role of the nurturer.

G: And accolades go to those women who play the role as
designed.

F: Our grandmothers and mothers were always giving. If it
wasn't a social club, it was a church or civic club. At church,
one group of women or another was always taking care of the
pastor, taking care of the sick and needy in the community.
Even during slavery, it was a case of taking care of someone.
Not just Whitefolks children. Taking in and caring for runaway slaves. Caring for the children of other slaves on the
plantation. Black women——all women——have always had to
put their arms around someone to nurture.

M: And that really is much like who we are. We represent a whole
lot of women. We're all very accomplished, but what we're not accom-
plished at is being able to say no. I think you're right when you say
women are socialized. But I don't think we can drop the ball and say
society dictates our behavior. Let's talk about Geneva, Bernadine's
mom, who's different from Robin's mom. How old is she?

Mt: She's 65. She's doing her own thing and doesn't jump
right in to help Bernadine. She waits to be asked. She even said

she didn't even like kids and wasn't interested in "doing that grandmother thing."

K: When you read about the kind of parent Geneva was, what was your perception of her?

B: This is a cool mom.

P: I think she was definitely a generation ahead of herself. I think those of us here who have daughters are more traditional than Robin's mom. We're professionals, and the fact that we're in a book discussion group is an indication that we're not like our moms...we're taking some time out for ourselves. I also think our daughters will be even less subservient than we are and even more concerned with their own well-being.

M: *Lets take a look at Savannah's mom. She's in Pittsburgh, has three other children, a daughter and two sons living with her, one of whom is always in trouble. She also has a horrendous marriage. What kind of mom is she?*

P: She's more typical. Because she's still caring for adult children. She's always there.

Mt: In a way, Savannah is taking care of her. Savannah takes care of important papers for her mother. Her mother is always asking Savannah to help the others out. What's interesting is that even though her mother and sister have had unsuccessful marriages, they're always trying to get a man for Savannah. And no matter how much success Savannah has, they thought she's a failure because she doesn't have a man.

P: We're back to that generation thing, thinking that you're not a complete woman unless you're married. That idea is changing.

K: Wasn't Savannah the dominant person, the most success

ful, the strong one in her family? Her mother and others felt they could impose anything on her, and they did. However, she allowed it to happen. Her mother would call and say, "Your brother just got out of jail, he needs money. He needs encouragement." Savannah was supposed to be the pick-up-person. "I can do it, mom. Just tell me whatever it is you need."

Mt: But mainly she was supportive from a distance. She wasn't excited to have her mother visit her.

F: I think it's because we're at different places emotionally. Savannah played the matriach and realized there was a dependency on her, but she didn't want to acknowledge that dependency.

M: *We've talked about the men as though they spring from Mars and somehow are not bound to us. I'd like to ask you if we tend to raise our daughters to be daughters and just love our sons and hope they get though it someway. Do we send them mixed messages? These men come from somewhere. The same mothers who have given us Bernadine and Savannah and Robin and Gloria, who are all very different, but strong, capable women, the same mothers gave us Troy, the drug dealer, and Michael.*

Mt: I have a son, but I didn't raise him to be like any of these men.

K: I'd like to think that the generations are changing, and that teaching self-love versus self-sacrifice is ending. Having two sons and a daughter, I'd like to think I've given my sons those nuturing instincts. One day those instincts will prove out.

B: I have a fifteen-year-old daughter who is quite sure of herself. Unless she changes radically, she won't need a man to validate her as a person.

P: Definitely! That's another discussion— how mothers raise their sons and daughters: the message mothers give their daughters, the message they give their sons, and the message that children receive by observing the relationships of the adults in their lives.

F: I think the book has lots of messages that we can all relate to in various ways.

B: I think Terry deliberately left it open. She deliberately didn't bring closure for the characters. I think she didn't resolve all those issues to give the reader something to think about.

P: The best part of the book, for me, is that it opened up discussion about sexuality and the social dynamic of personal relationships, among women, among men and women, among Black and White women, and between generations of women.

Provoking Discussion

Begin the discussion with "open-ended" questions. In other words, questions should be worded to solicit more than a "yes" or "no" answer. "What did you like or dislike about the book?" is much better than simply asking, "Did you like the book?"—unless you follow up by asking, "Why?"

You can also begin by discussing the title. How does it fit the story? Is it appropriate? What about the cover art? Is the cover relevant? Ask the group for cover suggestions. "How would you have

• • • • • • • • • • • • • •

The Black women's discussion group

is: Sisterhood! Spiritually!

Disagreement! Love! Enlightenment!

Education! & Bonding!

—*Roz Johnson*

• • • • • • • • • • • • • •

depicted the cover?" How was the cover a foreshadowing of the story? For example, the cover of *Falling Leaves of Ivy*, by Yolanda Jo, has what appears to be tire tracks superimposed over a college logo. Upon close inspection, the "tire tracks" are clearly skull and cross bones, which is definitely a foreshadowing of the story: murder. And the jacket of the hard cover version of Brent Wade's Company Man had an African ceremonial mask displayed. I'd suggest reading the poem "I Wear the Mask" by Paul Lawrence Dunbar prior to discussing this book.

- Often after giving a little background about the locale and the book's author, facilitators may ask: What is the book about? Relationships? About the main character's search for identity? Does it have a theme?

- What did you like or dislike about a particular character? Discuss that character's strengths and weaknesses.

- Discuss any one, or a number of, the relationships portrayed.

- Were there any surprises; turns of events?
- Was the outcome predictable?

- What was the turning point?
- At what point, if any, did the book become interesting? Why?

- At what point, if any, did it no longer hold your interest?

- How do you like the author's writing style? Would you like to read another book by this author? Does the author compare in any way to another? If this is not the author's first book, how does the writing compare to his or her other efforts?

Closing the Discussion

At what point does the facilitator put closure to the discussion? There are a few indications that it's time to end the discussion.

1. Time Is Up

   Facilitator should be aware of time. Approximately fifteen minutes prior to the end of thr alloted discussion time (one to two hours), the facilitator needs to ask discussants to give a summary the book.

2. Conversation lags.

   Facilitator should be aware that discussion has been exhausted and call for a summation from group or sum it up herself. If this happens long before the time expected, it's ok. The remainder of the time can be used to socialize. Group bonding is important. At one of our meetings, where only seven members showed up, half of them hadn't read the book, and two of the others had read half the book. The discussion lasted about twenty minutes, so we spent the rest of the time talking. Actually the conversation was monopolized by one member who shared some personal things that apparently she needed to talk about. But what was special was that she felt comfortable enough with the group to do so. We were happy to be there for her.

After the discussion, you might want to have each member write a brief comment about the book. The Go On Girl book club in New York has each of it's eighteen chapters read the same book at the same time. They critique the book, compile opinions and mail them to the author. The group considers this an important service to authors. Some authors have even written back.

Sister-to-Sister Guidelines

It's important to remind discussants that every statement is of value. If they don't understand, would like to disagree, or would like to take issue with a statement another person makes, they should be encouraged to do so. This democratic process is the heart of a discussion group. Whether or not you liked the book is less important. What's important is the discussion: what you thought about the characters, how the book made you feel. Discussion also provides an opportunity to see other perspectives and to get clarity on points not altogether understood when reading alone.

Personalities

Something to keep in mind: *All members are not the same.* Can you imagine how boring discussions would be if they were? The personalities and perspectives that each member brings makes for an interesting discussion.

As mentioned earlier, all members are not comfortable speaking out, in other words, interrupting. Don't be disappointed if some members are not as talkative as others. You'll find a few who tend to have strong opinions on every book, while others will have little to say. This diversity is the beauty of book discussion groups.

The spirit of sisterhood emerging in a discussion group is unparalleled. Why else would a member who hasn't read the book attend? Why else would members travel great distances in order to get to meetings?

A good group is one that provides an opportunity for each member to have a sense of belonging. It's one in which there is never a wrong interpretation; where every interpretation is valued. The message that a good discussion group conveys to its members is that the group is without question a circle of sisterhood.

Selecting a Fascilitator from the Group

Are there any volunteers? This method allows a member to facilitate a book about which they feel strongly about. However, it's the organizer or secretary's responsibility to keep track of who facilitated what and when, so that one person doesn't monopolize the facilitator's role.

Should everyone in the group take turns? In the BWLG, "Oh no, not me," is an unacceptble response when a member is asked to facilitate. Usually after a little encouragement, with other members even offering to help or co-facilitate, the person always agrees, and no one's ever needed a cofacilitator. The group's organizer, or secretary, should keep a list of facilitators as a way of making sure that everyone gets an opportunity to facilitate. No one should be allowed to refuse to facilitate.

Taking turns gives everyone an opportunity to participate, especially those who may not volunteer. In the BWLG, members volunteer or are volunteered. For certain books it's obvious that one member may be better at than another. For example: Kate, a very analytical member was asked to facilitate Paula Giddens' *When and Where I Enter*, a nonfiction book about women finding their own sense of themselves. Unfortunatley, it was too much like a text book and was not an enjoyable book to read. It turned out to be one of the best discussions we've had. The same with Iyanla Vanzant's *The Vaue in the Valley*. I knew that of all our members, Jaqui could best facilitate this book, and she did. Jaqui has an unusual ability to really see into a book. Rachel was asked to facilitate *Laughing in the Dark*, by Patrice Gaines (the story of a middle-class teenage girl who triumphs over a life of drugs, prison, and abuse), partly because she worked in a woman's shelter and through her job has seen many women who have emerged from adverse situations, and partly because Rachel, though she comes to every meeting, sits quietly, rarely offering input unless asked. This was an opportunity for us to see a different Rachel. She came prepared, making a comparison of the Gaines novel with Nathan McCall's *Makes Me Want to Holler* (also with a teenage protagonist), had a list of questions, and took charge, leading a spirited discussion. When this role was completed, Rachel once again became a good listener.

You Named It, You Claim It. The person who suggests the book gets to facilitate it. On the positive side, you'll probably get a facilitator who is eager to read and discuss the book. On the negative side, if there are members who can never come up with a book, they won't have an opportunity to facilitate, while others who are voracious readers, or who hear about good selections, will have many opportunities.

Having a Professional Facilitator

Some groups hire a professional facilitator. Unless perhaps for an annual meeting, where you may want to give all members an opportunity to enjoy the days' events equally, I don't see the need for a paid facilitator who is not a member of your group. Facilitating is not difficult, and, more often than not, most members are eager to talk about the book, and discussion usually flows smoothly. Very likely the professional facilitator will be viewed as an outsider because s/he doesn't know the group. S/he may not know, for instance, the loss a member has suffered through death, divorce, and could make a remark best presented differently. I think members in a book discussion group are special and would mostly consider a professional facilitator, except on a special occasion, an intrusion.

But there are groups out there that swear by the professional.

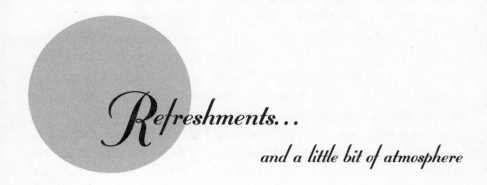

Refreshments...
and a little bit of atmosphere

While serving refreshments are not a must, they're always welcome. How much to spend will depend on where you meet—library, book store, restaurant, members' homes—and how members decide they want to handle it.

It's also fun to coordinate the locale in the book with the refreshments, and to create an atmosphere. When the B.W.L.G. read *R.L.'s Dream* by Walter Mosley, we had blues music playing in the background to set the mood. And when *Knowing*, by Rosalyn McMillan was read, we played Motown Hits, many of which were referred to throughout the book.

As far as decor is concerned, that's up to the individual. I encourage you to use your imagination. I think of my discussion group as guests in my home, and since I happen not to like paper plates and plastic utensils, we use china, my silver flatware, and crystal wine glasses. (Yes, we serve wine! We also serve water, coffee, and other beverages.) Because I hate doing laundry, I do yield to paper napkins, albiet nice ones. Using crystal stemware and china plates has absolutely no effect on the quality of the discussion. Members of the BWLG would enjoy their meeting just as much if I used paper plates. Because I love flowers, I also have fresh flowers on the diningroom table. Once when I forgot the flowers and was about to panic, I recalled that I'd read in B. Smith's cookbook that improvising is the key to hosting with ease. So, I went throughout the house collecting my African figures and cacti plants and arranged them stategically on the table. I also placed kente fabric runners horizontally across the table and sprinkled some of the sand that comes on top of the cacti pots on the table—creating an exotic atmosphere for a discussion of *Migrations of the Heart*, set in Nigeria. Another time, when I'd forgotten the flowers, I pulled petals from some roses that should have been discarded two days earlier, and sprinkled them across the table. This, too, was from B. Smith and was certainly a conversation piece.

When deciding what to serve, consider when you'll be eating; after the discussion, anything goes. If members are allowed to eat prior to and during, you may want to reconsider finger or drippy foods that may dirty the books. If you insist on chicken wings, or other foods that make for sticky fingers, have a basket of handi-wipes nearby.

It's better to have few small dishes of pretzels, or dip conveniently placed rather than one large bowl that members must constantly reach across to get. It can be disruptive if members are sitting in a circle repeatedly dipping during the discussion. It's not uncommon for an unthinking member to lean over directly in front of another who is making a point, to dip, or to reach for a handful of chips or pretzels.

Don't Forget the Fortune Cookies

If the spirit moves you, you can enhance your meetings by creating an ethnic ambiance that "rhymes" with the book the group is reading. If, for example, you are reading a book by a Chinese author, you could order some selections from a Chinese restaurant. Small touches add immeasurably to the atmosphere—enameled-chop sticks that members can take home; a "Chinese red" table cloth; lanterns or fans. Don't forget the fortune cookies!

For an African American theme, you could bake an Emancipation Proclamation Cake. There is a fool-proof recipe for this absolutely delicious cake in the Black Family Reunion Cookbook. Of course, corn bread and fried chicken would be appropriate, as would black eyed pea soup. (Recipes for all of the above and more can be found in the *B. Smith Cookbook*)

I found a delicious Native American Wild Rice Tart recipe and another for Ongwehowe Cookies on the Internet that came from the *Three Sisters Cookbook*.

For a Middle Eastern or Arabic theme, stuffed grape leaves or a rice pilaf—using basmati rice—go well with condinments such as cashews and raisins. You can make—or buy from your local Middle Eastern restaurant—a dip such as *hummus* to eat with pita bread or *tabouli* salad. If you really want to enhance the atmosphere, try adding Middle Eastern music! Most local libraries have a fairly wide range of ethnic music.

If you doubt the extent to which a people's music helps one culture *feel* the soul of another, imagine trying to "get into" Caribbean culture without a taste of Calypso music. Add a bit of Coconut bread, sea food, brightly colored napkins and a table cloth, a little sand...why, you could almost smell the ocean!

For a book set in Africa, try sending out a meeting notice just "mentioning" the fact that the discussion will end with "Gali Akpono" and coffee—if that does not peak your groups curiosity...! Prodigal members will be coming out of the woodwork just to see what Gali Akpono is! Since I've arouse your curiosity, I had better give you the recipe myself, instead of sending you off in search of yet another book.

• • • • • • • *Gali Akpono* * • • • • • • • •

1 cup white corn meal
2 eggs
1 1/2 cups flour
1/4 cup milk
3/4 tsp salt
1/2 tsp freshly grated nutmeg
4 oz. margerine

Dampen cornmeal with 2 TBS water. Add sugar, salt, and sifted flour. Mix in margerine; add lightly beaten eggs, reserving 1 egg white; add milk and mix. Add nutmeg. Roll dough out to 1/4" thickness, cut into 3" rounds. Mark edges with fork. Place on cookie sheet, brush tops with beaten egg white. Bake at 350 degrees for fifteen minutes, or until golden brown.

Lets not lose sight of the fact that food and ambiance, no matter how authentically ethnic, are not the most important ingredients. Many fine groups serve nothing more than water, coffee, tea, and soft drinks.

The most important ingredients for a discussion group are the people.

*From Monica Bayley's *Black African Cookbook,*
Determined Productions, San Francisco

Celebrations and Special Events

Book discussion groups go beyond sitting around talking about and dissecting books. The BWLG has hosted authors, taken a cruise, and, under the umbrella of the travel group Literary Sojourners, hosted theatre excursions. Every year we celebrate our anniversary with a Tea Party, where guests bring their favorite tea cup. The tea cups are on display for all to admire, as well as the books we've read during the past year. Then the original facilitators give a brief synopsis of their book, after which we vote on the books: best written, most fun, most inspiring, most erotic—you get the idea.

The Go On Girl Book Club from New York, established in 1992, holds an annual authors' awards ceremony. Surpassed only by the Oscar and Emmy Awards, the group presents an award based on votes by each of their twenty-two chapters to the Author of the Year and another to the Favorite First-Time Author.

Some groups have a book exchange. It's a great way to get rid of books that you don't want or to get something new to read.

As another idea, if there are members with craft skills, you might want to make a quilt depicting the books you've read.

Occasionally, the group may want to invite another group to jointly discuss a particular book. The discussion of the book *The Wedding* that I mentioned earlier was a collaboration of two groups. And, when a member of one group wrote a play, which contained parts for each member in her group, another group was invited to be the audience. This infusion of new people brings different perspectives, adds interest to the group, and is a way to meet new people.

Chapter 4

AUTHOR
APPEARANCES

• • • • • • • • • • • • • •

Meeting various

authors and being able

to discuss, listen and

absorb other view-

points are enriching

experiences.

—Liz Woodley

Supporting Ethnic Authors

Hosting author appearances is exciting and important for promoting writers. Unfortunately, ethnic authors are not sent on expenses-paid-tours as frequently as their White counterparts. Also, promotional dollars aren't as abundant for ethnic writers. In the *Quarterly Black Review*, Gwendolyn Parker, author of *These Same Long Bones* (an excellent book for discussion) wrote that: "...Sometimes African American book stores are mistakenly overlooked when tours are planned even though they are the very places that launch or maintain our careers." The consequences of this less than ambitious marketing is that it takes longer for folks to pass the word about new releases through "The Girlfriends' Network." Terry McMillan's quest for readers of her first book, *Mama*, is legendary. She took it upon herself to promote her book, writing thousands of letters to book stores and organizations. Her personal campaign was so sucessful that by the time the book was actually published, the first printing of her book was sold out, and within six weeks it was in its third printing. Though McMillan is definitely to be credited for her energy, the power of the The Girlfriends' Network cannot be discounted. The book was one you wanted to talk about.

However, too often, by the time readers find out about books via The Girlfriends' Network they're off the shelves, in remainder bins, and aren't scheduled for another printing. This is where book discussion groups can play a valuable role. *The Literary Connection*, published by the Black Women's Literary Guild, the *African American Reading Group Newsletter*, and the *Quarterly Black Review*, are just a few of the publications that inform, and link discussion groups whose member's are Black. Such publications are ways in which Black authors can be promoted. The Smithsonian is a good source for books by and about Native Americans. Try the Asia Society's book store obviously to find Asian writers. (See Appendices Book Sources). Book discussion groups can make a difference in the author's success. Remember, its not only important for you to hold a signing, but it's important for you to attend those held by others.

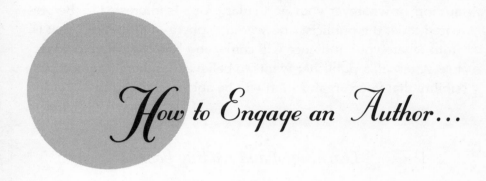

How to Engage an Author...

To engage an author, begin by contacting the publisher's publicity department as early as possible. Although author's tours are scheduled several months prior to the book's publication, call anyway. Then send your request in writing. Ask for a press release kit. And remember to write down the name of the publicist. You'll want to send a thank you note later. Develop a press release kit, and be prepared to make follow-up phone calls. Don't be discouraged. Be persistent until you get a definite "no."

Once I got a call from a publicist saying the author was coming to town to attend her college reunion. Because she was going to be in town for a couple of days, this ambitious author wanted to fill any spare moments promoting her book. I jumped at the opportunity. This led to another signing opportunity, where a friend was giving a party for the author and didn't want to handle the books. If the author is touring, there's no cost for their appearance. To avoid a surprise, always ask.

It won't hurt to write, on the group's letterhead stationary, a letter introducing your group to the publicist, informing him/her that your group is willing to host Black, Asian, Native American, Gay authors or whatever your particular group is interested in. Be prepared to let the publicist know your "sphere of influence," that is, from where your audience will come, and how you plan to advertise. After all, a publisher wants to believe that there's a good possibility that your organization will be able to attract guests.

• • • • • • • • • • • • • •

Learning of and reading books

that I probably would never have

known about and then engaging

in exciting discussions with

wonderful people are just a few of

the reasons why I enjoy my

discussion group.

—*Gertrude Cowan*

• • • • • • • • • • • • • •

Once a date has been confirmed, send invitations to everyone you know and to those you don't; don't forget social organizations. This is an opportunity to build a database for future use. Advertise in the "What's Happening" or "Upcoming Events" sections of local newspapers. Cable stations and some radio stations are also happy to make announcements. In terms of numbers, the more successful signing you host, the better your chances with the publisher of being given serious consideration in the future. The discount on books range from twenty-eight to fifty-percent, so signings can function as a fund raiser for the group's favorite cause or just as a way of building a slush fund.

Ordering the books

Because you'll probably be asked to pay for the books in advance, how far in advance to order is a judgment call. I'd suggest first calling the publisher to check on stock. In this way, you'll have some indication as to whether you should order immediately or can wait awhile. The decision is yours. Remember to ask the publisher about their return policy.

How many to order?

A rule of thumb is to order books for 1/3 of the number of guests you anticipate. This, again, is speculation. There are no attendance guarantees, and there is no guarantee as to how many of those present are going to buy, nor that they will buy at all. Another consideration: If this isn't the author's first book, you may want to have a few of her/his previous books available for sale.

Day of the Event

Here is a checklist of things to consider for the day
1. Have a guest book. This is a way to build a data base for future signings.
2. Have a comfortable table and a couple of pens, for the signing to take place.

3. At the podium, or speaker's table, have a small bottle of water and a glass. A flower or flowers will also add to the ambiance.

4. Before introducing the author, give a brief synopsis of his or her background, and accomplishments.

5. If the author is willing to personalize the book, I'd suggest giving guests paper on which to *print* the name to be inscribed. Trying to get the correct spelling of names can be quite a feat in a noisy room.

6. At the time of the signing, have one of the members of your group stand nearby to assist; to open the book, to take payment, to run interference between the author and overly talkative guests, etc. If possible, light refreshments are always welcome.

7. If there are a large number of people attending the event, and the author's arrival is delayed, you may want to give guests numbers in order of arrival. This way, those who arrive on time will be rewarded when it's time to get books autographed. It's good PR, and takes the edge off grumblers.

If the author doesn't show...

Regretfully, sometimes this can happen. It happened to me. I thought it was quite coup when Charlene Hunter-Gault's publicist scheduled her to make an appearance at an author signing we'd planned for her. This was a few years back, and Hunter-Gault was scheduled for a Friday evening. The room was reserved, the invitations sent, and the date written on many calendars. Unfortunately, on Thursday evening war erupted in Somalia, and during the day Hunter-Gault was assigned to cover the war. By sheer luck, I happened to stop by my house in the afternoon, only to hear the dreaded recorded message that apologetically informed me that she would not be able to make an appearance.

Since this was something over which I had absolutely no control,

I did what I could. As I said before, bibliophiles are wonderful people. Eveyone sympathized, drank wine, ate cheese and crackers, laughed, talked, and, after a few pleasant hours, departed.

Chapter 5

BOOK
COLLECTING

• • • • • • • • • • • • • • •

The spirit of sisterhood

is enough to join a

book discussion group;

reading and discussing

books is a bonus.

—Katherine Kennedy

The thing that makes books so special is that not only can you read them again and again, you can collect them, creating your very own library. Collecting is an interesting and exciting hobby, but it can be expensive once the collecting bug bites, and you've just got to have a particular book in order to complete a series. However, the personal reward you receive as your library develops is worth it. And, if you're lucky, the investment can be a profitable one.

There are many different reasons why people decide to collect books. Some people, usually referred to as bibliophiles, love books and can't part with them. Others hope that one, or more, of their books will increase in value. However, it seems that people of color are more interested in book collecting for the purpose of creating a legacy than for monetary reward.

Getting Started

S tart today! Preferably with First Editions. First Editions are books whose copyright date and date on the title page are the same, although books without title page dates can be First Editions. Another way to identify First Editions is that the copyright page only has copyright information. Being able to have complete series, or all the books written by an author, increases the value of your collection. So how do you find these books? Second-hand and out-of-print bookstores are always a good place to start, as are estate sales, auctions, and antiquarian book shows. Perhaps an elderly relative, or friend will let you peruse their collection in search of a few books that they know will be in the hands of someone who appreciates books as much as they do.

Predicting which books will become collectible (that is, those that will increase in value) is absolutely impossible. However, there are times when it appears that one book has more of a possibility of gaining value than another.

Erotique Noire is one such book. It is unique because it's the first collection of Black erotica written by acclaimed novelists, poets, scholars, and essayists to be published.

Books by authors who become famous are also a good investment. One astute collector found a first edition of *Once*, the first book by Alice Walker, for which he paid $1.00. The book has since been given a value of $300.00. Keep an eye out for First Editions. The First Edition of *The Color Purple, Jonah's Gourd Vine, Brown Girl, Brownstone,* and the *Bluest Eye* are rare because they were published in small quantities.

Although a library copy or a Book-of-the-Month (BOMC) edition may complete your series, unless autographed, they don't have appreciable resale value and are not recommended for serious collectors. BOMC editions can usually be identified by a small star on the back cover. Also, there is never a price listed on the jacket of a BOMC issue. Be advised, first editions of BOMC issues may be labeled First Editions, so don't confuse them when you intend to collect trade books.

Books being collected for future monetary value should:
- be in their original jackets to have the most value. (Every cloth book published in America after 1930 has a dust jacket. The absence of a book jacket decreases value, as does a jacket that is not in "MINT" condition.)
- not be a "Book Club" edition.
- be in the best condition possible; referred to literally as "MINT."
- not be packed too tightly or too loosely in bookcases.
- not be exposed to sunlight or to prolonged exposure to fluorescent light.

- not be placed face down with other books on top, and nothing thicker than a bookmark should be used to mark your place in a book.

Because of the proliferation of titles, some collectors advise choosing sub-specialties. For example, you may want to collect only novels, or biographies, autobiographies, or perhaps mysteries, or gay/lesbian writings. Collecting books by authors of color is relatively new. So, if you're thinking about building a library that has potential value, any of these is probably a good specialty.

When browsing yard sales or used book shops keep in mind the story told by Charles Blockson, curator at the Blockson Collection at Temple University, who picked up a book thought to be *Roots,* by Alex Haley, that turned out to be a copy of *Uncle Tom's Cabin* by Harriet Beecher Stowe. I suppose the moral of that story is not to judge a book by its cover.

Occasionally, a book will be deemed "priceless." Such a book is a copy of *Lincoln: The Unknown,* written in 1930 by Dale Carnegie, bound in the skin of a Black man. The book is currently preserved in a glass case at Temple University in Pennsylvania. There's also reported to be a book of poetry by Phillis Wheatly that's "bound in the skin of a Black girl."

Appendices

A Historical Look at Book Discussion Groups

Though forming organized book discussion groups appears to be a 1990s phenomenon, women have for generations been meeting to discuss books. In the nineteenth century, however, these groups were called literary circles or societies, the purpose was the same: to read, discuss, enlighten, and bond.

During the nineteenth century, free women of color were not welcomed to White organizations. Undeterred, these women formed their own literary, debating, and abolitionist societies, focusing on self-development through the study of books, art, literature, history, music, or philosophy.

Discussion groups were popular among free women of color throughout the antebellum. Though formed primarily for the purpose of self-enrichment and furthering abolitionist causes, the agenda for these groups included literary discussions. After 1830, the lines of demarcation among moral reform movements, political protest groups, mutual beneficial societies, secret lodges, insurance associations, library companies, and literary societies became difficult to discern. That is, though the words "literary society" may be in the groups' name, their primary concerns may have been other than literary.

In a speech before the American Moral Reform Society, in 1787, Philadelphian sailmaker James Forten reported knowledge of several literary societies. He commented that he was, "Gratified to see so large a number in one grand purpose: the diffusion of knowledge, and to hear them reading and reciting in a manner that would reflect honor upon the community."

Prior to emancipation in 1863, Blacks who were already enjoying the privilege of being free men and women formed societies to encourage literary and intellectual development, although abolitionist activities were most always on the evenings' agenda. Many abolitionists met under the "guise" of intellectual meetings. Members of literary or debating societies were so deeply involved in abolitionist activities that this involvement has been stated as a possible cause for the decline, at least for a while, of literary societies. A report in the American Anti-Slavery Society stated that:

> *The various anti-slavery organizations weakened the strength of literary and debating societies in that they called constantly on the members of the literary societies to furnish audiences for their lectures and that leaders in these societies were pressed into service as speakers and workers for the emancipation programs. Among those who were members and officers of literary and anti-slavery societies, were: William Whipper and Robert and Harriet Purvis.*

Although books were not readily accessible, nor easily attainable in non-free states prior to the Civil War, free

Blacks met to discuss whatever was available. Often, according to the following report, it was the bible:

Soon after all were quietly seated a short address prepared for the occasion was read by the author Sarah Douglass. The fifty-four beautiful and encouraging chapters of Isiah was then read. After sitting a short time under a solemn and impressive silence that ensued the reading of this chapter, one of the company vocally petitioned our Heavenly Father for a continuation of His favor. The remainder of the evening was spent affecting slave tales, calculated to bring forcibly into view, the deplorable situation of your fellow creatures in the south, both the oppressor and the oppressed.

These literary foremothers were usually married, high school graduates, and employed in professional occupations ranging from elocutionists and musicians to seamstresses and milliners, though in some cases they were domestics and laundresses.

Judging from the following post-war journal entry of a member of a Northern literary society, book discussion groups of today haven't changed much, except that music then was live, as opposed to compact disks; and personal essays have given way to books purchased from book stores housing multi-volume works.

From the first month of our marriage, Mr. Fleetwood and myself have reserved Thursday evening to receive our friends—we are happy to see them at any time but obligate ourselves to be at home on Thursday. We adopted the following program which has proved satisfactory: 1. Music, 2. Reading, followed by conversation on the same, then an Essay and conversation on the Essay, after which, answers to questions proposed at a previous meeting, followed by questions to be answered at the next meeting. The chairman [now called a facilitator] of the evening then announces the Essayist and Reader for the next week. This is followed by a quotation recited by

*each one present. The closing exercise is music. One distinctive fea-
ture of these evenings is the well understood fact that no refreshments will be furnished, a decision that does much to insure the per-
manency of these entertainment*

The efforts of literary societies of the late eighteen and early nine-
teen hundreds deserve recognition and praise, for they not only
helped to disseminate knowledge among people, for the most part
poorly educated, but they also taught the Negro [their term] how
to use his leisure time to advantage. Lecturers who addressed these
societies chose not only literary topics but also scientific and educational ones, prompting Blacks who could read to read further,
and those unable to read to learn to read.

As a result of the literary activities of these early societies, many
Blacks established private libraries. David Ruggles, a printer and
abolitionist, is the earliest known Black to collect books focusing on
the experience of Black people. His book store was located at
Lispenard St. in New York. Ruggles maintained a lending library
containing anti-slavery and colonization publications. For a fee of
less than twenty-five cents, books could be rented for a year.
Unfortunately in 1835, Ruggles' book store/library was destroyed
by a White mob.

Knowing about these early literary societies is important according to the late Dorothy Porter, author and archivist at Howard
University:

*Early Negro literary societies, are indications of the activity of self-
educative influences in Negro life; invaluable because they were frequently the background for the organization of the Negro school.
They were the supporters of the educative life among Negroes in a
day when there were few formal instruments of education in exis-
tence for their use.*

Porter's argument is futher strengthened by Northeastern University Professor Maryemma Graham, who tells us that:

Knowing of these groups is a strong indication of an active intellectual life among Black people, and it is extremely unfortunate that we do not have any more information about them.

Literary societies in general provided a forum through which women became informed about issues and skilled in effecting change. There were often poetry readings and musical performances. Some even offered experiences with parliamentary procedures, opportunities to develop leadership skills unhampered by either male or White dominance. Most provided increased educational awareness of racial issues that included segregation in transportation and voting rights. Many Black literary societies often adopted projects to benefit their race, using fundraising to support local homes for the aged, colored schools, or orphanages. Larger literary groups usually convened in churches or other public locations open to Blacks.

The evening's program usually included reading the classics, including William Shakespeare. Biographies of notables of the day like Phyllis Wheatley and Toussaint L'Ouverture were especially enjoyed. Frequently, well-known speakers Frederick Douglass, Richard Grenner, Mary Church Terrell, and Booker T. Washington were invited.

Early literary societies were especially important for the Black professional class women. Concerned with their intellectual development, these women were themselves either professionals, i.e. beauticians, dressmakers, teachers, etc., or were married to men of professional status, i.e., caterer, undertaker, or teachers, etc. Josephine Turpin Washington, best known for her activities in various civic and social organizations, summed up the sentiment of this privileged group in the following quote: "Even the society woman, usually adept at what is known as 'small-talk,' needs an opportunity to cultivate conversation that rises above the gossip of the drawing room and the inanities that too often mark the social whirl."

In the early 1900s, President Franklin Delano Roosevelt instituted the Works Project Administration, commonly referred to as the WPA. This project provided funds for promising artists and writers, freeing them to create, without financial worry. Because of the WPA, Langston Hughes and Zora Neale Hurston, among others, flourished and became notable writers of this period known as the Harlem Renaissance. So prolific were the Black Literati that many "took for granted that the intellectual center of Afro-America was located above Central Park," in Harlem.

Throughout the 1920s, a reading and discussion group, led by a Miss Ernestine Rose, was held at New York Public Library's Harlem Branch, now the site of the Schomburg Center for Research in Black Culture. Among the wealth of historical documents at the Schomburg are the ashes of author/poet, Langston Hughes, which are buried in the floor of the foyer.

The following section introduces chronologically several literary societies that existed in this country between the early 1800s and 1900s.

PENNSYLVANIA

Philadelphia is not only noted for being the location of the first-known literary society established by Blacks in this country, but it seems to have been the home for many other literary societies.

Here are the names and missions of a few, with whatever details that are known about them.

The **Benjamin Banneker Society,** named after the famous astronomer/mathematician, sponsored lectures on political, scientific, religious, and artistic issues

The **Female and Literary Society** of Philadelphia, had the unique distinction of being the first Black women's literary society. In 1831, the society had twenty members who met every Tuesday evening for the purpose of "mental improvement in moral and literary pursuits." Members wrote original plays, short stories, and essays that were anonymously placed in a box, and later critiqued by members.

The **Gilbert Lyceum**, formed for literary and scientific purposes, is believed to be the first society to admit both males and females. Although only twelve were present at an organizing meeting held on January 31, 1841, membership in the Lyceum quickly increased to forty-one members, among whom were anti-slavery activists Robert Purvis and Sarah Mapp Douglass.

The **Minerva Literary Association** was founded in 1834 by thirty women who wanted to establish a real school for the encouragement and promotion of polite literature. At weekly meetings members enjoyed readings and recitations of original and selected pieces, together with appropriate matters.

The **Philadelphia Library Company of Colored Persons** "aimed to be of service to the entire population of the city." It was formed by nine free Blacks on New Year's Day in 1833. The primary objective of the group was to build a collection of books on every subject for the benefit of its members, and to enlighten the group by means of weekly lectures on literary and scientific subjects. Within three years, membership had increased so tremendously that the group decided to incorporate. Members paid a one-dollar membership fee and were assessed twenty-five cents a month. From the first week in October to May, the group hosted lectures given by members and guests at St. Thomas Episcopal Church.

The **Reading Room Society**, organized in Philadelphia some-time around 1828, is reported to have been the first. Founded espe-cially for young men, the group met weekly, listing the need to be of good morals as a primary qualification for membership. With monies collected from dues and initiation fees, the group pur-chased books to build a library.

The **Theban Literary Society** in Pittsburgh was founded in 1831 by Louis Woodson, an African Methodist Episcopal minister.

The **Young Men's Literary and Moral Reform Society of the City of Pittsburgh and Vicinity** was founded in 1837. Objectives of this organization were pretty much the same as other literary soci-eties of the times. Welcomed at monthly meetings were young men between the ages of eighteen and thirty-five who demonstrated the ability to pay a monthly fee of twelve and a half cents, and who were of "known moral habits and respectability." Editor and author Martin Delany was selected as librarian for the group.

In her book *Philadelphia's Black Elite*, professor and author Julie Winch writes that "young men were urged to form literary soci-eties to improve the mind and contradict allegations of intellectual inferiorities."

NEW YORK

The **Ladies Literary Dorcas Society of Rochester** and The **Young Ladies Literary Society of Buffalo** were established in 1836. The Lit-Mu-Club, a literary club founded in 1922, was concerned not only with reading and discussing books, but with charitable work. During Black history week, the group set up special exhibits at the library, and other locations in Buffalo. The **Lit-Mu-Club** is credited with introducing Negro History Week to Buffalo. Charlotte Hawkins Brown, Mary Church Terrell, and poet Countee Cullen were among the club's guest speakers.

The **New York African Clarkson Society** was established in

New York City in 1829 for young men who were Free persons, in good health, of moral character, between the ages of twenty-one and forty, and who would not, in any probability, become a charge to the society. The society's fifth anniversary was celebrated at Harlem's renowned Abyssinia Baptist Church.

The **New York Female Literary Society**, aka **The Ladies Library Society of the City of New York**, was established in 1834. To support their community outreach projects, the women held fairs to raise money for causes such as *The Colored American*, a newspaper, and the New York Vigilance Committee.

The **New York Philomathean Society**, founded in 1834, was considered New York's leading literary society, "devoted to the improvement of literature and useful knowledge." By 1837, the society had acquired over six hundred books for its lending library. An admission fee was charged for lectures on literary and historical subjects at their twice-weekly meetings.

The **Phoenix Society**, established in 1834, had the largest membership and was the most influential. At the time the society was founded it was the only institution in New York organized primarily for colored youth. Potential members were required to be of good moral character, between the ages of four and twenty. The membership fee was twelve and a half cents, and dues were one cent per week. At their meetings, main topics of discussion for the over one-hundred-and-fifty young people in attendance was singing, praying, and reading of original compositions.

The **Ladies' Literary Society of New York** was established in 1854. Members were not unlike other literary societies in the mid-eighteen hundreds, where membership was restricted to the elite of the Black community; wives and daughters of ministers, teachers, and businessmen.

MASSACHUSETTS

The **Adelphic Union for the Promotion of Literature and Science** was organized in December of 1836. The group met in a rented hall outside the colored settlement in the central part of the city. This location was attractive to non-Blacks and many attended meetings. In turn, White societies invited Blacks to attend their meetings.

The **Afric-American [sic]Female Intelligence Society**, of Boston, founded in 1832, has the distinction of being the first of its kind in Massachusetts. This progressive feminist group dared to sponsor abolitionist Maria Stewart, who spoke before an audience of men and women. Her engagement was considered a bold move because during this time neither Black nor White women were allowed to speak on political subjects at public meetings. Prospective members of the society had to be accepted by majority vote. Members were fined twenty-five cents when absent. Concerned with the welfare of their own, the group gave ailing members, with a minimum of a years' membership, one dollar a week to help sustain them.

The **Boston Literary and Historical Association** was formed in 1901 "to foster intellectual life and debate among prosperous African Americans." The group met every two weeks, from October to May, then weekly from December to February at the Prince school, located just outside the Black community. Open to the public, meetings were attended by both Blacks and Whites. William Monroe Trotter, publisher and editor of *The Guardian*, was a founder.

The **Boston Philomathean Society**, was formed in 1836 to promote literature and to establish a library. The society's meetings were held at the Center Street Chapel.

St. Mark Musical and Literary Union, organized in 1902, had as its main concern, "to foster intellectual life and debate among prosperous African Americans." Unlike the Boston Literary and Historical Association, St. Marks met within the community at the church, which was then located in Boston at 1042 Tremont St. Their meetings were held from October to May on Sunday afternoons.

The **Young Men's Literary Society** organized in 1845, in order "to improve their minds, strengthen their intellectual faculties and cultivate a refined literary taste among the young men of the community."

MARYLAND

Prior to 1865, locations within slave territory, Baltimore and Washington, D.C., were not ideal for the development of literary pursuits among Blacks. Here free Blacks were more concerned with issues of survival, primarily maintaining their free status.

Although free, Blacks were nevertheless subjected to "Black Laws" that restricted their movement. These laws could forbid Blacks from attending school, joining organizations, and even from walking in the streets at night. Free Blacks were required to carry a pass, being caught without it would most likely mean enslavement, whether they were born free or not.

Approximately 1,500 of the 25,000 free Negroes living in Baltimore, in 1830, were thought to be members of one organized group or another. Unfortunately, very little information is available specifically about literary societies in Baltimore and Washington, D.C.

In addition to the societies listed below, we know that around 1835, there existed **The Young Men's Mental Improvement Society for the Discussion of Moral and Philosophical Questions of all Kinds** and the **Phoenix Society**.

The **Baltimore Literary and Historical Association**, another elite society, was organized at the Bethel AME Church, "in the interest of all the people." This society represents the visibility of Baltimore's emerging Black social and cultural organizations before WWI.

The **Monumental Literary and Scientific Association** founded in 1885 consisted of a number of the city's most prominent citizens. Attracting only "the best classes of our citizens," the **Monumental** was "the pride and glory of educated Baltimorians."

WASHINGTON, D.C.

The **Female Literary Society**, founded around 1834, was like other African American women's literary societies in northern cities, in that it combined educational activities with abolitionist concerns. High on the priority list for this group was raising funds to assist runaway slaves and donating money to support a petition campaign aimed at ending slavery in Washington, D.C.

Other clubs, about which nothing beyond name and date of inception are known, are The **Mu-So-Lit-Club** and **The Washington Conventional Society.**

ARKANSAS

Fifteen years prior to the emancipation, in 1863, of slaves, forty-percent of Blacks in Arkansas were free. In Little Rock, Black upper-class communities enjoyed opportunities not available to their less fortunate brothers and sisters. Two organizations were there, the **Lotus** and the **Bay View Reading Clubs**, both important centers for musical and literary activities.

MISSOURI

The **Forum Club**, an affluent club in St. Louis with 186 members, was able to purchase their own building.

The **Idle Hour Literary Society** had among their membership some of St. Louis, Missouri's aristocracy of color such as the Langstons and Vashons. Organized in 1886, the society met throughout the year, except in summer, for monthly programs that included musical performances and literary study.

ALABAMA

The **Tuskegee Women's Club** was founded with thirty-five members in 1895, and within one year's time membership had increased to seventy-four. At semi-monthly meetings, members critiqued readings, reviewed articles, and discussed diverse, intellectual topics such as the value of the x-ray, wireless telegraph, famous women of the hour, and the use of electricity in medical science.

MINNESOTA

Members of St. Paul's **Adelphia Club**, founded as a literary and philanthropic organization in 1899, were a select group of women. To remain exclusive, new members to the organization were recruited only from daughters of charter or existing members.

LOUISIANA

In 1860, New Orleans, members of **The Athenaeum Club** met weekly in New Orleans to "hear papers on literature and politics."

The **Iroquois Literary and Social Club**, while appearing to be a social and literary club was in reality a forum for Republican activities.

The **Monday Night Literary Club** invited guest speakers such as poet, educator, and rights activist Charlotte Forten Grimke, and Black leader and orator Frederick Douglass.

The **Saturday Evening Club** hosted literary scholars of the day. In the early part of the twentieth century, the **Woman's Club** of Baton Rogue, established in 1890, met weekly "for the purpose of fostering sociability, doing literary work and planning receptions and socials."

OHIO

Prior to the emancipation, in 1863, Blacks in Ohio were more concerned with drawing up of resolutions to petition the Ohio Legislature for repeal of laws depriving them of "those rights which pertain to citizenship" than enjoying the leisure of formalized literary societies. Here, although Blacks paid taxes that were allocated for public schools, their children didn't have the privilege of free and public school education. With these conditions to combat, it's understandable that literary societies weren't prolific. Although in 1835, in a report given at the Ohio Anti-Slavery Society, mention is made of a lyceum in Cincinnati, where lectures on scientific and literary subjects were presented twice weekly to an audience of between one hundred-fifty to three-hundred people.

The **Ohio Literary Ladies Education Society** was "devoted to promoting a proper cultivation for literary pursuits and improvements of the facilities and powers of the mind" In addition to providing forums for discussing relevant issues, they established private libraries, organized debating societies, held poetry readings, helped needy women, and gave financial aid to Black newspapers.

In the 1900s, Cleveland's literary clubs benefited by having among their guests the esteemed author Charles Chestnutt. However, many literary societies were far more social than literary. **The Georgia Douglas Johnson Literary Society**, named for the poet and author, and the **Saturday Night Neighbors**, are remembered as being "as lively as a saloon."

MICHIGAN

Most members of the **Detroit Study Club**, formed in 1898, were Black school teachers and leaders. Booker T. Washington was just one of the club's distinguished guest speakers.

Literary Terms

Afrocentrism   Philosophy whose roots are from Africa.

Allegory   Figurative treatment of one subject, under the guise of another; symbolical narrative.

Antagonist   Character or force in conflict with a main character or protagonist.

Anecdote   Short, entertaining retelling of life experience(s).

Anticlimax   Noticeable descent in speaking or writing from lofty ideas or expressions to commonplace remarks.

Antihero   One who would be considered the hero were it not for his or her unfavorable actions.

Autobiography   A form of nonfiction in which a person tells his or her own story.

Biography   A form of nonfiction in which a writer tells the life story of another person.

Character   Person or animal who takes part in the action of a literary work. Characters are sometimes classified as round or flat, dynamic or static. A round character shows many traits, faults as well as virtues.

Climax   A story's highest point of interest or suspense.

Conflict   A struggle between opposing forces. Characters in conflict form the basis of stories and novels. There are two kinds of conflict: external and internal.

Copyright   The publisher's or author's exclusive right of use for a specified number of years.

Copyright date   Date copyright is granted.

Dialect   The form of a language spoken by

people in a particular region or group.

Dialogue   Conversation between characters; used to reveal characters and to advance action.

Epic   A long poem that tells a story, usually about a hero.

Essay   Short nonfiction work about a par ticular subject. There are four types of essays:
a) *Descriptive essay*   Seeks to convey an impression about a person, place, or object;
b) *Narrative essay*   Tells a true story;
c) *Expository essay*   Gives information, discusses an idea, or explains a process;
d) *Persuasive essay*   Tries to con vince readers to do something or to accept the writers point of view.

External conflict   Main character struggles against an outside force.

Fable   Short tale, usually using animals, that is written to teach a moral.

Fiction   Prose writing that tells about an imaginary character and events.

Figurative language   Writing or speech not meant to be interpreted literally; i.e., as fact.

First edition   An edition that denotes printing from the original type set, regardless of years between printing,or number of times book has been printed.

Flashback   A section of a literary work that interrupts the sequence of events to relate an event from an earlier time.

Foil   A character who is contrasted with another character.

Folklore   Stories woven around myths of a particular culture.

Folktale   A short narrative passed down through generations.

Foreshadowing   Clues that suggest events to come.

Framework story   Text that contains a story within a story.

Genre   A division or type of literature. There are three major genres: poetry, prose, and drama. Each major genre is further divided.

Griots   In Africa, the keepers and tellers of stories; preservers of the oral tradition.

Hero   Male character whose actions are inspiring or noble.

Heroine	Female character whose actions are inspiring or noble.
Idiom	Dialect or style of speaking that's particular to people of a region.
Internal conflict	Involves a character in self-conflict.
Irony	Literary technique that involves differences between appearances and reality, expectation and result, or meaning and intention.
Limited edition	A small specified number of books printed.
Literal language	Interpreting words as fact.
Main character	Most important charter in a story, often changing in some important way as a result of the story's events.
Metaphor	Likening two unrelated things to one another.
Mood, or atmosphere	A feeling created by a literary work or passage.
Moral	A lesson taught through a literary work.
Motif	Recurring subject, theme, or idea.
Narrative	A telling of events as reported by a

person, or persons; can be fiction or nonfiction.

Narrator

Speaker or character who tells a story; can be a character in the story or an outside observer. The writer's choice of narrator determines the story's point of view.

Negritude

French-language literary movement based on the concept of a shared cultural bond on the part of Black Africans and their descendants wherever they may be in the world. The word is believed to have originated in 1953.

Nonfiction

A story based on facts.

Novel

A lengthy literary work of fiction containing a plot thatexplores characters in conflict. May have one or more subplots, or minor stories and several themes.

Oral tradition

Passing along of stories from one generation to another, by word of mouth.

Parody

Humorous or satiracal interpretation of a serious work.

Pathos

Writing that evokes pity or compassion.

Plot	Sequence of events in a literary work; usually begins with an *exposition* that introduces the setting, the characters, and the basic situation. An incident follows that introduces the *central conflict*. The conflict increases during development until it reaches a high point of interest or suspense; the climax. All events leading up to the climax make up the *rising action*, followed by the *falling action*.
Point of view	Opinion, ideas of a particular person.
Prose	One of the major genres of literature that occurs in two forms: fiction and nonfiction; most common form of the written language.
Protagonist	Main character in a literary work.
Protest fiction	Speaks out against social injustice.
Realism	Fiction writing that is true to life.
Satire	Style of writing that uses humor to criticize people, ideas, or situations in hopes of improving them.
Setting	Time and place of the action; historical period—past, present, or future—but also a specific year, season, or time of day. Place may involve not only the geographical

place—a region country, state, or town—but also the social, economic, or cultural environment.

Short story

A brief work of fiction. In most short stories, one main character faces a conflict that is worked out in the plot of the story.

Simile

Figure of speech in which two unlike things are compared.

Slave narrative

First-hand autobiographical accounts by Black Americans describing their experiences as slaves.

Stream of consciousness

Written exactly as thoughts flow from the mind.

Surreal

Dreamlike. Makes readers question whether characters are imagining events, or whether events are actually happening.

Tone

The writer's attitude toward his or her audience and subject; formal, informal, serious, playful, bitter, or ironic.

Tragedy

Literature dealing with somber themes culminating in a tragic conclusion.

Unabridged

Complete text of a book. The opposite

is abridged; i.e. condensed.

Verisimilitude   The appearance of truth or realization (i.e. real life experiencews or events) in a work of fiction; a writer, creates "verisimilitude" by giving characters realistic traits, mannerisms, speech, etc.

Voice   Essence or quality of expression unique to a particular author or character.

Zeitgeist   Characteristic of a particular time period; general trend of thought.

Literary Awards to People of Color...for Fiction & Non-fiction

AMERICAN BOOK AWARD / BEFORE COLUMBUS FOUNDATION

Recognizes literary achievements by people of various ethnic backgrounds.

1980 Rudolfo Anaya (Chicano) *Tortuga*
1980 Leslie Marmon Silko (Native American) *Ceremony*
1980 Quincy Troupe (African American) *Snake-Back solos*
1981 Toni Cade Bambara (African American) *The Salt Eaters*
1983 Barbara Christian (African American) *Black Women Novelists*
1983 Joy Kogawa (Japanese Canadian) *Obasan*
1983 Alice Walker (African American) *The Color Purple*
1984 Amari & Amina Baraka (African American) *Confirmation:An Anthology of African American Women*
1984 Paule Marshall (African American) *Praisesong for the Widow*
1985 Sandra Cisneros (Chicana) *House on Mango Street*

1985 Louise Edrich (Native American-German / American) *Love Medicine*

1986 Gloria Anzaldúa (Chicana) & Cherrie Moraga (Chicana) *This Bridge Called My Back*

1987 Aná Castillo (Chicana) *The Mixquiahuala Letters*

1987 Terry McMillan (African American) *Mama*

1988 Toni Morrison (African American) *Beloved*

1989 Isabel Allende (Chilean) *Eva Luna*

1989 J. California Cooper (African American) *Homemade Love*

1989 Alma Luz Villanueve (Chicana) *The Ultraviolet Sky*

1990 Paula Gunn Allen (Native American) *Spider Woman's Granddaughter*

1990 Quincy Troupe (African American) *Miles: The Autobiography*

1990 Shirley Geok-lin Lim (Chinese American) *The Forbidden Stitch: An Asian American Women's Anthology*

1990 Hualing Nieh (Chinese American), Mayumi Tsutakawa (Japanese American) *Mulberry and Peach: Two Women of China*

1990 Itabari Njeri(African American) *Every Good Bye Ain't Gone*

1991 Mary Crow Dog (Native American) *Lakota Woman*

1991 Jessica Hagedorn (Phillipino) *Dogeaters*

1991 Joy Harjo (Native American) *In Mad Love and War*

1991 John Edgar Wideman (African American) *Philadelphia Fire*

1992 Raymond Andrews (African American) *Jessie and Jesus* [and] *Cousin Claire*

1992 A'Lelia Perry Bundles (African American) *Madam C.J. Walker:Entrepreneur*

1992 Shelia Hamanaka (Japanese American) *The Journey*

1992 Edward P. Jones (African American) *Lost in the City*

1994 Graciela Limón (Chicana) *In Search of Bernabe'*

1994 Jill Nelson (African American) *Volunteer Slavery*

1995 Robert L. Allen (African American) *Brotherman*

1995 Herb Boyd (African American) *Brotherman*

1995 Li-Young Lee (Chinese American) *The Winged Seed: A Rememberance*

1995 Linda Raymond (African American) *Rocking the Babies*

AMERICAN ACADEMY AND INSTITUTE OF ARTS AND LETTERS

Given for encouragement and achievement in art, music, and literature.

1970 James A. McPherson (African American) *Hue and Cry*
1973 Alice Walker (African American) *In Love & Trouble*
1978 Toni Morrison (African American) *Tar Baby*
1981 David Bradley (African American) *The Chaneyville Incident*

NATIONAL BOOK AWARD

Instituted in 1949, honoring distinctive works of fiction that depict American intellectual life.

1957 James Baldwin (African-American) *Giovanni's Room*
1976 Alex Haley (African American) *Roots*
1983 Alice Walker (African American) *The Color Purple*
1987 Amy Tan (Chinese American) *The Joy Luck Club*
1989 Oscar Hijuelos (Cuban American) *The Mambo Kings Play Songs of Love*
1990 Charles Johnson (African American) *Middle Passage*

NATIONAL BOOK CRITICS CIRCLE AWARD

Recognizes books by American authors, written in English, by members of the National Book Critics Circle.

1976 Maxine Hong Kingston (Chinese American) *The Woman Warrior*
1977 Toni Morrison (African American) *Song of Solomon*
1984 Louise Erdich (Native American-German / American) *Love Medicine*
1988 Toni Morrison (African American) *Beloved*
1988 Bharaï Mukherjee (Indian) *The Middleman and Other Stories*
1993 Ernest Gaines (African American) *Lesson Before Dying*

The NOBEL PRIZE for LITERATURE

International prize, regarded as the highest recognition awarded for the total literary output of a distinguished writer.

1968 Yasunari Kawabata (Japanese)
1982 Gabriel García Márquez (Columbian)
1986 Wole Soyinka (Nigerian)
1988 Naguib Mahfouz (Egyptian)
1990 Octavio Paz (Mexican)
1992 Derek Wolcott (St. Lucian)
1993 Toni Morrison (African American)
1994 Kenzaburo Ōe (Japanese)

O'HENRY AWARD

Recognizes the year's best short story published by American authors in American periodicals.

1944 Frank Yearby (African American)
1987 Louise Erdich (Native American-German / American) *Love Medicine*

PEN FAULKNER AWARD

Honors the best work of fiction published by American authors in a calendar year.

1981 David Bradley (African American)*The Chaneysville Incident*
1983 John Edgar Wideman (African American) *Sent for You Yesterday*
1990 John Edgar Widemen (African American) *Philadelphia Fire*

PULITZER PRIZE

Established with funds willed by journalist Joseph Pulitzer, awarded annually for the American novel, published during the year which best presents "the whole atmosphere of American life, and the highest standard of American manners and manhood."

1969 N. Scott Momaday (Native American) *House Made of Dawn*
1978 James Alan McPherson (African American) *Elbow Room*
1983 Alice Walker (African American) *The Color Purple*
1988 Toni Morrison (African American) *Beloved*
1990 Oscar Hijuelos (Cuban American) *The Mambo Kings Play Songs of Love*

SCIENCE FICTION WRITERS OF AMERICA

Promotes the art of science fiction writing.

1966 Samuel R. Delany (African American) *The Einstein Intersection*
1967 Samuel R. Delany (African American) *Babel-17*.

Recommended Reading

THE CIRCLES OF SISTERHOOD

• • • • • • • • • • • • •

Suggestions for

reading 'n

discussion ...

AFRICAN

1958	Things Fall Apart	F	Chinua Achebe	Nigeria / Late 1880s Colonialism / Turn of century / Human spirit
1964	Arrow of God	F	Chinua Achebe	Nigeria / 20th century / Abuse of power / Colonialism /
1976	The Bride Price	F	Buchi Emecheta	Nigeria / Modern women vs. traditional roles / Dominated Dowry
1979	Joys of Motherhood	F	Buchi Emecheta	Three generations / Ibo women / Changing values regarding child rearing
1981	Ake	M	Wole Soyinka	Nigeria / Author's child-

A=Autobiography / B=Biography / F=Fiction / NF=Nonfiction / M=Memoir / SS=Short-Stories / SF=SciFi / R=Romance / AN=Anthology
*(Semi-Autobiographical)

				hood/Early education/Memories of his mother
1981	The Beggars' Strike	N	Aminata Sow-Fall	Senegal/Beggars/Strike
1981	So Long a Letter	F*	Mariama Bâ	Senegal/Mature woman writes to younger woman: their husbands' taking 2nd wives/Women's dilemma
1986	Black Sisters, Speak Out	NF	Awa Thiam	Black Africa/Feminism/Opression/Polygamy/Clitoridectomy
1987	Anthills of the Savannah	F	Chinua Achebe	W.Africa/Politics/Sacrifice/Three friends
1992	The Famished Road	F	Ben Okri	Africa/Social life/Magic
1993	Songs of Enchantment	F	Ben Okri	Sequel to The Famished

A=Autobiography / B=Biography / F=Fiction / NF=Nonfiction / M=Memoir / SS=Short-Stories / SF=SciFi / R=Romance / AN=Anthology
*(Semi-Autobiographical)

Year	Title	Type	Author	Description
1994	*Kehinde*	AN	Buchi Emecheta	Road/Africa/England/Endurance
1994	*African Rhapsody*	SS	Nadezda Obradovic	African authors
1994	*Long Walk to Freedom*	A	Nelson Madela	Comtemporary African short stories
1994	*Of Water and Spirit*	F	Patrice Malidoma Some	Political activist/First Black President of S. Africa
1994	*Unwinding Threads*	SS	Charlotte Bruneri, ed.	Initiation of an African shaman/Rites/Ceremonies
1995	*Zenzele*	F	J.Nozipo Maraire	African/Women
				Letters from Zimbabwe mother to her daughter attending Harvard

A=Autobiography / B=Biography / F=Fiction / NF=Nonfiction / M=Memoir / SS=Short-Stories / SF=SciFi / R=Romance / AN=Anthology
*(Semi-Autobiographical)

AFRICAN AMERICAN

Year	Title		Author	Description
1851	*Incidents in the Life of a Slave Girl*	A	Harriet Jacobs	Slave narrative/1820s-1840s/South/NewYork/Boston
1898	*Four Girls at Cottage City*	F	Emma D. Kelly-Hawkings	Martha's Vineyard/Four young women/Sisterhood
1900	*House Behind the Cedars*	F	Charles Waddell Chestnut	Post Civil War/North Carolina/Romance/Color consciousness
1928	*Quicksand*	F	Nella Larsen	Mulatto woman/Identity
1929	*The Blacker the Berry*	F	Wallace Thurman	Early 1900s/Idaho, LA, NY/Color complex
1932	*The Conjure Man Dies*	F	Rudolph Fisher	Detective/Mystery/Harlem/1930s

A=Autobiography / B=Biography / F=Fiction / NF=Nonfiction / M=Memoir / SS=Short-Stories / SF=SciFi / R=Romance / AN=Anthology
*(Semi-Autobiographical)

Year	Title		Author	Description
1937	*Their Eyes Were Watching God*	F	Zora Neale Hurston	Rural Florida/Early 1900s Folklore/Romance/Survival
1946	*The Street*	F	Ann Petry	Suburban Connecticut/Harlem/Single parent survival
1948	*The Living Is Easy*	F*	Dorothy West	1930s Boston/Middle class/Controlling, devoted father
1953	*The Narrows*	F	Ann Petry	1950s/Connecticut/Interracial relationship
1956	*Proud Shoes*	M	Pauli Murray	Successful African American family/Pre-& post-Civil War
1965	*Autobiogrphy of Malcolm X*	A	Malcom X and Alex Haley	Civil Rights Activist/Nation of Islam/1920s to 60s

A=Autobiography / B=Biography / F=Fiction / NF=Nonfiction / M=Memoir / SS=Short-Stories / SF=SciFi / R=Romance / AN=Anthology
*(Semi-Autobiographical)

Year	Title		Author	Description
1966	*Jubilee*	F*	Margaret Walker	South/Pre- & Post--Civil War/Slavery/Black mistress
1969	*The Bluest Eye*	F	Toni Morrison	Ohio/Young black girl wants blue eyes/Incest/Racism/Self-esteem/Identity
1969	*The Chosen Place, the Timeless People*	F	Paule Marshall	Caribbean/Interraction between oppressed and the oppressors
1971	*Autobiography of Miss Jane Pittman*	F	Ernest Gaines	Experiences in Deep South of a 100-year-old woman
1973	*Sula*	F	Toni Morrison	Midwest/Friendship/Infidelity/Survival
1974	*Angela Davis*	A	Angela Davis	Ex-Black Panther/Activist/Professor

A=Autobiography / B=Biography / F=Fiction / NF=Nonfiction / M=Memoir / SS=Short-Stories / SF=SciFi / R=Romance / AN=Anthology
*(Semi-Autobiographical)

Year	Title		Author	Description
1977	*Song of Solomon*	F	Toni Morrison	Late 1800s-Early 1900s/Michigan/Materialism/Family
1979	*Kindred*	F	Octavia Butler	SciFi/Los Angeles & Antebellum South/1800s/1976
1981	*The Chaneysville Incident*	F	David Bradley	Historical realism/1930 to 1970s/Philadelphia, Virginia
1982	*The Color Purple*	F	Alice Walker	South/Two sisters corre spond:subjugation of women in Africa and in America/Abuse/Survival/Love/Faith
1982	*Women of Brewster Place*	F	Gloria Naylor	Mid-60s/Urban/Abuse/Extended family/Love/survival

A=Autobiography / B=Biography / F=Fiction / NF=Nonfiction / M=Memoir / SS=Short-Stories / SF=SciFi / R=Romance / AN=Anthology *(Semi-Autobiographical)

Year	Title		Author	Description
1983	A Gathering of Old Men	F	Ernest Gaines	South/Unity/Terror/Triumph/Elderly men
1983	Migrations of the Heart	A	Marita Golden	African husband/American wife/New York/Culture clash-African/American
1983	Praisesong for the Widow	F	Paule Marshall	New York/Caribbean/Middle-class materialistic 60-ish widow/Search for self
1984	Brothers & Keepers	A	John Edgar Wideman	One son a Rhodes Scholar/Another in prison/Family relationships
1985	Linden Hills	F	Gloria Naylor	Early 1980s/Suburb/Northern city/Middle class/Intrigue
1987	After the Garden	F	Doris Jean Austin	Love/Abuse/Family/

A=Autobiography / B=Biography / F=Fiction / NF=Nonfiction / M=Memoir / SS=Short-Stories / SF=SciFi / R=Romance / AN=Anthology
*(Semi-Autobiographical)

1940s/Survival

Year	Title	Type	Author	Description
1987	Beloved	F	Toni Morrison	Historical realism/Post-Civil War/Ohio/Escaped slave haunted by her dead infant
1987	Mama	F*	Terry McMillan	Michigan/LosAngeles/Family/Togetherness/Survival
1988	Mama Day	F	Gloria Naylor	Conjure woman/Tradition/Love/Sea Islands
1988	A Woman's Place	F	Marita Golden	Four friends from teens to adulthood/Life experiences
1989	Baby of the Family	F	Tina McElroy Ansa	Georgia/1940s/Psychic powers/Family relationshps
1989	Disappearing Acts	F	Terry McMillan	Lovers/Rejection/Social

A=Autobiography / B=Biography / F=Fiction / NF=Nonfiction / M=Memoir / SS=Short-Stories / SF=SciFi / R=Romance / AN=Anthology
*(Semi-Autobiographical)

				Incompatibility
1989	Long Distance Life	F	Marita Golden	D.C./Multi-generational relationships/Survival/
1989	Women of Brewster Place	F	Gloria Naylor	Seven desparate women all living on a dead-end street, a metaphor for their lives
1989	Yamilla	F	Mildred Riley	Historical romance/Africa/The south/Multi-generational
1990	Devil in Blue Dress	F	Walter Mosley	First/Easy Rawlings mystery/L.A./1948
1990	Middle Passage	F	Charles Johnson	New Orleans/Slave ship/Free Blacks/1830s
1991	All-Bright Court	F	Connie Porter	Buffalo, New York/

A=Autobiography / B=Biography / F=Fiction / NF=Nonfiction / M=Memoir / SS=Short-Stories / SF=SciFi / R=Romance / AN=Anthology *(Semi-Autobiographical)

Year	Title		Author	Description
				Migration North/Survival
1991	Family	F	J. California Cooper	Slavery/Survival/Mother's ghost
1992	Baily's Cafe	F	Gloria Naylor	Cafe and it's patrons/Some bizarre life stories
1992	Company Man	F	Brent Wade	Corporate world/Glass ceiling/Struggle for survival
1992	Dead Time	F	Eleanor Taylor Bland	Female detective/Texas/Love/Mystery/Murder
1992	Falling Leaves of Ivy	F	Yolanda Jo	Yale U/New York/Murder/Suspence/Interracial romance
1992	In My Place	A	Charlayne Hunter-Gault	Journalist/First Black

A=Autobiography / B=Biography / F=Fiction / NF=Nonfiction / M=Memoir / SS=Short-Stories / SF=SciFi / R=Romance / AN=Anthology
*(Semi-Autobiographical)

Year	Title	Type	Author	Themes
				female to enter attend U. of Georgia
1992	*Invisible Life*	F*	E. Lynn Harris	Homosexuals/Hetrosexual/Compassion
1992	*Jazz*	F	Toni Morrison	Harlem/1920s/Bittersweet love/Revenge
1992	*Soul to Soul*	A	Yelana Khanga	Black Russians/America/Jewish/Roots
1992	*Waiting to Exhale*	F	Terry McMillan	Male-female relationships/Professionals/Arizona/Sisterhood
1992	*Your Blues Ain't Like Mine*	F	Bebe Moore Campbell	Mississippi/Racism/Murder/Relationships
1992	*Tapping the Power Within*	NF	Iyanla Vanzant	Spiritual Development/

A=Autobiography / B=Biography / F=Fiction / NF=Nonfiction / M=Memoir / SS=Short-Stories / SF=SciFi / R=Romance / AN=Anthology
*(Semi-Autobiographical)

Year	Type	Title	Author	Description
				Afrocentric/Self-help/Inspirational
1993	F	Chesapeake Song	Brenda Richardon	Virginia Middle class/Love & Disappointment/Sacrifice
1993	M	Days of Grace	Arthur Ashe	Tennis star/AIDS/Discrimination
1993	SS	Forty-three Septembers	Jewelle Gomez	Lesbian writers from several ethnicities
1993	F	Her Own Place	Dori Sanders	Struggles/Survival/Faith
1993	A	Having Our Say	Bessie & Sadie Delany	100 years of persoanl history told by two sisters who lived it/No. Carolina/NY
1993	B	King of the Cats	Wil Haygood	Adam Clayton Powell, Jr./Activist/Minister

A=Autobiography / B=Biography / F=Fiction / NF=Nonfiction / M=Memoir / SS=Short-Stories / SF=SciFi / R=Romance / AN=Anthology *(Semi-Autobiographical)

Year	Title		Author	Description
1993	A Lesson Before Dying	F	Ernest J. Gaines	South/1930s/Teaching/Learning dignity
1993	Pushed Back to Strength	M	Gloria Wade-Gayles	Professor at Spellman College
1993	This Little Light of Mine	B	Kay Millis	Life. of Civil Rights Activists Fanny Lou Hamer
1993	Ugly Ways	F	Tina McElroy Ansa	Three sisters/Family relationshps/Death/Self-identity
1994	Black Gold	F	Anita Richmond Bunkley	Texas 1846-1950/Romance/Adventure/Oil fields/Wealth
1994	Black Betty	F	Walter Mosley	Mystery/L.A./White man/Congressman

A=Autobiography / B=Biography / F=Fiction / NF=Nonfiction / M=Memoir / SS=Short-Stories / SF=SciFi / R=Romance / AN=Anthology
*(Semi-Autobiographical)

Year	Title		Author	Description
				in search of Black mistress hires Black detective Easy Rawlings
1994	*The Black Christ*	NF	Kelly Brown Douglas	A woman's perspective of Christ
1994	*Brothers and Sisters*	F	Bebe Moore Campbell	Corporate world/Survival/Blacks/Whites/Relationshps
1994	*Colored People*	M	Henry Louis Gates, Jr.	Harvard professor/Scholar/Writer/Peidmont W. Virginia
1994	*Fatheralong*	NF	John Edgar Wideman	Father-son relationships/1940s-90s
1994	*Fragments of the Ark*	F	Louise Merriweather	So. Carolina/Slaveship/Sea adventure/Escape/Historical/Romance

A=Autobiography / B=Biography / F=Fiction / NF=Nonfiction / M=Memoir / SS=Short-Stories / SF=SciFi / R=Romance / AN=Anthology
*(Semi-Autobiographical)

Year	Title		Author	Themes
1994	Gal	M	Ruthie Bolton	South/Incest/Hardships/Struggle to survive
1994	Gone Quiet	F	Eleanor Taylor Bland	Female Detective/Love/Mystery/Murder
1994	In Search of Satisfaction	F	J. California Cooper	Multigenerational/Post-Civil War/Struggle between God & the devil/Power/Greed/Love
1994	Makes Me Wanna Holler	A	Nathan McCall	Virginia inner city/Gangs/Supportive family
1994	The President's Daughter	F	Barbara Chase-Riboud	Pre- & post-Civil War/Thomas Jefferson & mistress-slave Sally Hemings
1994	The Serpent's Gift	F	Helen Elaine Lee	Midwest/Extended family/Survial

A=Autobiography / B=Biography / F=Fiction / NF=Nonfiction / M=Memoir / SS=Short-Stories / SF=SciFi / R=Romance / AN=Anthology
*(Semi-Autobiographical)

Year	Title	Type	Author	Description
1994	*Sisters and Lovers*	F	Connie Briscoe	Three sisters/Search for meaningful relationships
1994	*These Same Long Bones*	F	Gwendolyn Parker	North Carolina/Middle class/Togetherness/Tragedy/Survival
1994	*When Death Comes Stealing*	F	Valerie Wilson Wesley	Female Detective/Love/Mystery/Murder
1995	*Afrekete*	AN	Catherine McKinley & Jane Delaney, eds.	Contemporary Black Lesbian writings
1995	*The Between*	F	Tananarive Due	Upper middle class/Urban North/Relationships/Suspense/Surrealism
1995	*Crossing Over Jordan*	F	Linda Beatrice Brown	Civil War/Early 1900s/Mother-daughter relationship

A=Autobiography / B=Biography / F=Fiction / NF=Nonfiction / M=Memoir / SS=Short-Stories / SF=SciFi / R=Romance / AN=Anthology *(Semi-Autobiographical)

Year	Title	Type	Author	Description
1995	*Somebody Else's Mama*	F	David Haynes	Missouri/Middle class/Family conflict
1995	*The Sun, the Sea, a Touch of Wind*	F	Rosa Guy	Haiti/Romance
1995	*The Wedding*	F	Dorothy West	South/Slavery/Martha's Vineyard/Class & color consciousness
1996	*The Devil's Hatband*	F	Robert O. Greer	1996/Colorado/Suspense/Bounty hunter
1996	*Don't Block the Blessings*	A	Patti LaBelle	Diva of song/Revelations of her life
1996	*Go the Way Your Blood Beats*	AN	Shaun Stewart Ruff, ed.	Black writers (some notable)/Lesbian & gay/Historical & contemporary
1996	*The Hand I Fan With*	F	Tina McElroy Ansa	Sequel to *Baby of the Family*/

A=Autobiography / B=Biography / F=Fiction / NF=Nonfiction / M=Memoir / SS=Short-Stories / SF=SciFi / R=Romance / AN=Anthology
*(Semi-Autobiographical)

Year	Title		Author	Description
				Love/Sex/Life-affirming/Conjuring
1996	*Knowing*	F*	Rosalyn McMillan	Marital relationships/Upward mobility/Detroit/1990s
1996	*Life on the Line*	A	Faye Wattleton	President of Planned Parenthood/Womens' Rights activist
1996	*Live at Five*	F	David Haynes	Television news anchor/Awarness/The Ghetto/Relationships
1996	*Maker of Saints*	F	Thulani Davis	Mystery/Murder/Friendship/New York/Art world
1996	*Prophet of Rage*	B	Arthur J. Magida	Life of Louis Farrakhan

A=Autobiography / B=Biography / F=Fiction / NF=Nonfiction / M=Memoir / SS=Short-Stories / SF=SciFi / R=Romance / AN=Anthology
*(Semi-Autobiographical)

Year	Title		Author	Description
				Nation of Islam
1996	Push	F	Sapphire	Inner city teen/Abuse/Self-awareness/Learning to read/Education
1996	Season of Beento Blackbird	F	Akosua Busia	One man/Three women who love him/Caribbean/New York/Ghana
1996	Seven League Boots	F	Albert Murray	Adventures of touring bass player
1996	Shade	AN	Bruce Morrow & Charles Rowell, eds.	Ficton by gay men of African descent
1996	Stealing Home	M	Sharon Robinson	Baseball great Jackie Robinson's daughter/Celebrity life/Father-daughter relationship

A=Autobiography / B=Biography / F=Fiction / NF=Nonfiction / M=Memoir / SS=Short-Stories / SF=SciFi / R=Romance / AN=Anthology
*(Semi-Autobiographical)

Year	Title		Author	Description
1996	*Starlight Passage*	F	Anita Richmond Bunkley	Historical fiction/Mystery/Search for legacy/1800s-1990s
1996	*Tumbling*	F	Diane McKinney-Whetstone	So. Philadelphia/1940s-60s/Community/Personal relationships
1996	*Waking from the Dream*	A	Sam Fulwood III	Black middle class/1945-69/Cultural assimilation

A=Autobiography / B=Biography / F=Fiction / NF=Nonfiction / M=Memoir / SS=Short-Stories / SF=SciFi / R=Romance / AN=Anthology
*(Semi-Autobiographical)

ASIAN

Year	Title	Type	Author	Description
1975	*Junglee Girl*	SS	Ginu Kamani	India / Eleven stories / Sexual freedom / Opression
1988	*The Satanic Verses*	F	Salman Rushdie	India / Good & evil / Myths / Islam
1989	*The Joy Luck Club*	F	Amy Tan	Pre 1949 Chinese women / First generation American daughters / Cultural difficulties
1991	*The Kitchen God's Wife*	F	Amy Tan	China / Family / Legacy / Two generations
1991	*The Chinese Western*	SS	Ihu Hong	Contemporary fiction
1991	*Jasmine*	F	Bharti Mukher Jee	India / N.Y. / Iowa

A=Autobiography / B=Biography / F=Fiction / NF=Nonfiction / M=Memoir / SS=Short-Stories / SF=SciFi / R=Romance / AN=Anthology
*(Semi-Autobiographical)

Year	Title	Type	Author	Description
				Relationships/Cultural identity
1991	Woman in the Dunes	F	Kobo Abe	Japan/Intrigue/Self-imposed isolation/Alienation
1993	Farewell My Concubine	F	Lilian Lee	Peking Opera/Two male opera singers/One in female roles/From apprenticeships to professionals/On-stage lovers & backstage private lives
1993	The Holder of the World	F	Bharati Mukherjee	1670/India/America/Interracial affair
1993	The Remains of the Day	F	Kazoui Ishiguro	English butler/Reflections on pre- & post-war British Empire & ruling class/

A=Autobiography / B=Biography / F=Fiction / NF=Nonfiction / M=Memoir / SS=Short-Stories / SF=SciFi / R=Romance / AN=Anthology *(Semi-Autobiographical)

Year	Title		Author	Description
				Romance as told by Japanese writer
1994	*Blood Into Ink*	NF	Miriam Cooke, ed.	South Asia/Middle Eastern women/War stories
1994	*Obasan*	F	Joy Kogawa	Historical/Japanese Canadian/Reparation
1995	*American Knees*	F	Shawn Wong	Chinese-American/Japanese-Irish/Traditions
1995	*A Bridge Between Us*	F	Julie Shigekuni	San Francisco/Japanese-Americans/Four generations
1995	*On Gold Mountain*	NF	Lisa See	Los Angeles/Chinatown/100-year history/Chinese-American

A=Autobiography / B=Biography / F=Fiction / NF=Nonfiction / M=Memoir / SS=Short-Stories / SF=SciFi / R=Romance / AN=Anthology
*(Semi-Autobiographical)

Year	Title	Type	Author	Keywords
1995	*The Hundred Secret Senses*	F	Amy Tang	China/San Francisco/Family/SisterRelationships/Betrayal
1995	*My Own Country*	M	Abraham Verghese	India/Ethiopia/Tennessee/1985/Doctor
1995	*The Samurai's Garden*	F	Gail Tsukiyama	Japanese/History 1926-45
1995	*Spring Snow*	F	Yukio Mishmia	Tokyo/Aristocracy/Romance/1900s
1996	*Among the White Moon Faces*	M	Shirley Lim	Asian/American/Culture Conflicts
1996	*Dark Ring of Murder*	F	Misa Yamamura	Tokyo/N.Y./Murder/Mystery
1966	*The Garlic Ballards*	F	Mo Yan	Epic/China/Communist

A=Autobiography / B=Biography / F=Fiction / NF=Nonfiction / M=Memoir / SS=Short-Stories / SF=SciFi / R=Romance / AN=Anthology
*(Semi-Autobiographical)

Year	Title	Type	Author	Description
1996	Middle Son	F	Deborah Iida	Japanese-American / Culture struggle
1996	Mona in the Promised Land	F	Gish Jen	Chinese / Upper-middle class / Scarsdale, N.Y. / Cultural assimilation
1996	Moon Cakes	F	Andrea Louie	China / Romance / Ohio / N.Y. / Search for self
1996	Night, Again	SS	Linh Dihn, ed.	Contemporary short stories by Vietnamese
1996	Novel Without a Name	F	Thu Hunong Duong	Viet Nam / War
1996	Snow Country	F	Yasunari Kawabata	Geisha / Wealthy suitor / Tragic affair
1996	The Sorrow of War	F	Bao Ninh	Vietnamese war / North Vietnamese

A=Autobiography / B=Biography / F=Fiction / NF=Nonfiction / M=Memoir / SS=Short-Stories / SF=SciFi / R=Romance / AN=Anthology
*(Semi-Autobiographical)

| 1996 | Still Life with Rice | F | Helie Lee | Korea/Grandmother/Ancestors |
| 1996 | Tiger's Tail | F | Guss Lee | Korea/1974/Scandal/Judicial corruption/Chinese American |

A=Autobiography / B=Biography / F=Fiction / NF=Nonfiction / M=Memoir / SS=Short-Stories / SF=SciFi / R=Romance / AN=Anthology
*(Semi-Autobiographical)

CARIBBEAN

Year	Title		Author	Description
1986	When Rocks Dance	F	Elizabeth Nunez-Harrell	Trinidad/Turn of the century/Inner-struggles
1992	Tree of Life	F	Maryse Condé	Panama Canal/America/Multi-generational
1994	Ballard for a New World	SS	Lawrence Scott	Passion/Betrayal
1994	Breath, Eyes, Memory	F	Edwidge Danticat	Haiti/America/Family/Abuse/Self-worth
1994	The Emigrants	F	George Lamming	Barbados/1950s/Migration
1994	If I Could Write This in Fire	AN	Pamela Maria Smorkaloff, ed.	Literature from the Carribean

A=Autobiography / B=Biography / F=Fiction / NF=Nonfiction / M=Memoir / SS=Short-Stories / SF=SciFi / R=Romance / AN=Anthology
*(Semi-Autobiographical)

Year	Title	Type	Author	Description
1994	A Small Gathering of Bones	F	Patricia Powell	Jamaica/Homosexuality
1994	Spirits in the Dark	F	Nigel Thomas	Homosexuality/Repression
1995	All Soul's Rising	F	Madison Smart Bell	Haiti/Revolution/Toussaint
1995	Crossing the Mangrove	F	Maryse Condé	Guadeloupe/Love/Murder/Relationships/Conflict
1995	Sleep on Beloved	F	Cecil Foster	Jamaica/Imigrants/Women/America
1996	Seasons of Dust	F	Ifeona Fulani	Caribbean/London/Family and cultural conflicts

A=Autobiography / B=Biography / F=Fiction / NF=Nonfiction / M=Memoir / SS=Short-Stories / SF=SciFi / R=Romance / AN=Anthology *(Semi-Autobiographical)

LATINA/LATINO

Year	Title		Author	Description
1988	*And We Sold the Rain*	F	Rosario Santos, ed.	Contemporary fiction from Central America
1988	Love in the Time of Cholera	F	Gabriel García Márquez	So. America/Turn of century/Love triangle/Middle aged lovers
1991	*How the Garcia Girls Lost Their Accents*	F	Julia Alvarez	Dominican Americans/Sisters/Culturalization
1991	*House on Mango Street*	F	Sandra Cisneros	Chicago barrio/Seeking the American dream
1991	*Puerto Rican Writers at Home*	AN	Faythe Turner	Seventeen Puerto Rican men & women authors
1991	*Infinite Plans*	F	Isabel Allende	Anglo Hispanic/View of

A=Autobiography / B=Biography / F=Fiction / NF=Nonfiction / M=Memoir / SS=Short-Stories / SF=SciFi / R=Romance / AN=Anthology
*(Semi-Autobiographical)

Year	Title		Author	Keywords / Setting
				America
1991	*Kiss of the Spiderwoman*	F	Manuel Puig	Homosexuality/Politcal revolution/Relationships/Prison
1992	*Cantora*	F	Sylvia Lopez-Medina	Multi-generaltional/Mexican/American/Love/Family secrets
1992	*Dreaming in Cuban*	F*	Cristina Garcia	Mother & daughters/N.Y./Cuba
1992	*Like Water for Chocolate*	F	Laura Esquivel	Mexico/Romance/Recipies/Home remedies
1987	*Road to Tamazunchale*	F	Ron Arias	Magic/Realism/Fantasy
1992	*The Year of the Death of Ricardo Reis*	F	Jose Saramago	1936/Portugal/Brazil

A=Autobiography / B=Biography / F=Fiction / NF=Nonfiction / M=Memoir / SS=Short-Stories / SF=SciFi / R=Romance / AN=Anthology
*(Semi-Autobiographical)

Year	Title		Author	Description
1993	Growing Up Latino	M	H. Autenbaum and I. Stevens, eds.	Memoirs and stories of Chicano and Hispanic culture
1993	When I Was Puerto Rican	M	Esmeralda Santiago	Puerto Rico/New York/Cultural identity
1994	A Darker Shade of Crimson	F	Rubin Navarielle,JR.	Havana/Brooklyn/Sisterhood/Independence
1994	Poncho	F	Jose Antonio Villarrel	Mexican/Americans
1995	Act of the Damned	F	Antonio Lobo Antunes	Portugal/Humor/Shock/Wealth
1995	Boriquas	AN	Roberto Santiago, Ed.	Forty 19th & 20th century Puerto Rican writers
1995	Cactus Blood	F	Lucha Corpi	Female Detective/Chicanos/Migrantworkers/California

A=Autobiography / B=Biography / F=Fiction / NF=Nonfiction / M=Memoir / SS=Short-Stories / SF=SciFi / R=Romance / AN=Anthology
*(Semi-Autobiographical)

Year	Title		Author	Description
1995	*Cure for Evil*	F	Rafael Yglesias	Cuba/Psychoanalyst/ Bi-racial theme
1995	*In the Time of Butterflys*	F	Julia Alverez	Domenican Republic/ Truijillo/Escape/New life
1995	*Out of the Mirrored Garden*	F	Delia Poey, ed.	New fiction by Latin American women
1995	*Zia Summer*	F	Rodolfo Anya	New Mexico/Mystery/ Detective
1996	*America's Dream*	F	Esmeralda Santiago	Westchester County, N.Y./ Puerto Rican nanny/ Mental abuse
1996	*Our Lady of Babylon*	F	John Rechy	
1996	*Streets of Fire*	F	Soledad Santiago	Puerto Rican mother/ Survival/Children

A=Autobiography / B=Biography / F=Fiction / NF=Nonfiction / M=Memoir / SS=Short-Stories / SF=SciFi / R=Romance / AN=Anthology
*(Semi-Autobiographical)

1996	The Secret of the Bulls	F	Jose Bernard	Love/Pre-revolutionary Cuba
1996	Tijuana	SS	Federica Campbell	Tijuana, Mexico
1996	Under the Feet of Jesus	F	Helena Maria Viramontes	Mexican-Americans/Values
1996	Yo!	F	Julia Alavarez	One woman/Five perspectives of the Dominican Republic

A=Autobiography / B=Biography / F=Fiction / NF=Nonfiction / M=Memoir / SS=Short-Stories / SF=SciFi / R=Romance / AN=Anthology
*(Semi-Autobiographical)

NATIVE AMERICAN

Year	Type	Author	Title	Notes
1969	F	N. Scott Momaday	*House Made of Dawn*	Southwest / WWII / 1945 / Culture clash / self-love
1981	F	Martin Cruz Smith	Gorky Park	Soviet Union / America / Intrigue / Mystery written by Seneca Yaqui-Isleta Pueblo Native American
1985	F	N. Scott Momanday	*The Ancient Child*	Indian Lore / Adoption / culture / identity
1988	SS	ed. Beth Brant	*A Gathering of Spirit*	Collection by North American Indian Women
1990	F	James Welch	*Indian Lawyer*	Cultural identity / Blackmail by Blackfeet author

A=Autobiography / B=Biography / F=Fiction / NF=Nonfiction / M=Memoir / SS=Short-Stories / SF=SciFi / R=Romance / AN=Anthology
*(Semi-Autobiographical)

Year	Title		Author	Description
1990	*Lakota Woman*	A	Mary Crow Dog	Sioux / / Early 1970s / Tradition / Feminist movement
1990	*Medicine River*	F	Thomas King	Blackfeet Reservation / Alberta, Canada / Realism / Humor
1990	*Spiderwoman's Granddaughter*	AN	Paula Allen Gunn, ed.	Native American women writers
1991	*Almanac of the Dead*	F	Leslie Marmon Silko	Pueblo / Extended Family / History / Relationships / Drugs
1991	*The Crown of Columbus*	F	Michael Dorris	Anthropology / Satire / Romance / Christopher Columbus diary
1993	*Love Medicine*	F	Louise Erdrich	Native American / Culture /

A=Autobiography / B=Biography / F=Fiction / NF=Nonfiction / M=Memoir / SS=Short-Stories / SF=SciFi / R=Romance / AN=Anthology
*(Semi-Autobiographical)

				Conflicts
1991	*Sharpest Sight*	NF	Louis Owens	Choctaw/Chicano/Roots/Murder
1992	*Almanac of the Dead*	F	Leslie Marmon Silko	Pueblo/Extended family/History/Drugs/Relationships
1993	*Mankiller: A Chief of Her People*	A	Wilma Mankiller	Chief of Cherokee Nation
1993	*Love Medicine*	F	Louise Erdrich	Native American/Culture/Conflicts
1994	*Death of Sybil Bolton*	F	Dennis McAuliff, Jr.	Osage Indian/Murder/1920s
1995	*Messengers of the Wind*	NF	Jane Katz, ed.	Native American life stories/Customs

A=Autobiography / B=Biography / F=Fiction / NF=Nonfiction / M=Memoir / SS=Short-Stories / SF=SciFi / R=Romance / AN=Anthology
*(Semi-Autobiographical)

1995	*Solar Storms*	F	Linda Hogan	Multigenerational/Native American/Women/Struggles
1996	*Dance for the Dead*	F	Thomas Perry	Murder/Theft/Native American guide
1996	*A Gathering of Spirit*	SS	ed. Beth Brant	Collection by North American Indian Women
1996	*Hawk Woman Dancing with the Moon*	NF	Tela Starhawk Lake, ed.	The last female shamas
1996	*Sun Dancer*	F	David London	Native American community/Alcoholism/Medicine Man
1996	*Pushing the Bear*	F	Diane Glancy	Cherokee/Historical fiction/Trail of Tears

A=Autobiography / B=Biography / F=Fiction / NF=Nonfiction / M=Memoir / SS=Short-Story / SF=SciFi / R=Romance / AN=Anthology
*(Semi-Autobiographical)

Year	Title		Author	Notes
1966	*The Sun Is Not Merciful*	SS	Anna Lee Walters	Navajo/Arizona/ Contemporary tribal life
1996	*The Wind Is My Mother*	NF	Bear Heart	Life and Teachings of a Native American shamus

A=Autobiography / B=Biography / F=Fiction / NF=Nonfiction / M=Memoir / SS=Short-Stories / SF=SciFi / R=Romance / AN=Anthology
*(Semi-Autobiographical)

OTHER WRITERS OF COLOR

Year	Title		Author	Description
1992	*Beirut Blues*	NF	Hanan al-Shaykh	Arab woman's search for self/Civil strife/Lebanon
1993	*Arab and Isreal for Beginners*	NF	Ron David	History of Arab-Israeli conflict/Documentary comic book
1993	*Remembering Babylon*	F	David Malouf	Australia/Aborginies/1840s/British/New identity
1994	*Blood into Ink*	NF	ed: Miriam Cooke	South Asian/Middle Eastern Women/War stories
1994	*The Future of the Gulf*	NF	Feisal Al-Mazidi	The legacy of war and the challenges of the 1990s
1996	*The Moor's Last Sigh*	F	Salaman Rushdie	A Moor in India/Dubious

A=Autobiography / B=Biography / F=Fiction / NF=Nonfiction / M=Memoir / SS=Short-Stories / SF=SciFi / R=Romance / AN=Anthology
*(Semi-Autobiographical)

character/Passion/Greed/Seduction/Mysteries of art

| 1996 | Drops of This Story | M | Suheir Hammad | Young Arab refugee/Teens to womanhood/Black neighborhood in Brooklyn |

A=Autobiography / B=Biography / F=Fiction / NF=Nonfiction / M=Memoir / SS=Short-Stories / SF=SciFi / R=Romance / AN=Anthology
*(Semi-Autobiographical)

Directory of Book Discussion Groups

Book Discussion Group	Year Founded	Membership Gender	No. of	Dues	Meeting Date/Time	Member Intake
Black Women's Literary Guild Contact person: Pat Neblett Address: Twenty-eight Hart Cir. Randolph, MA. 02368 Phone: (617) 961-4164 FAX: (617) 296-4949	1992	F	20	$25/yr.	3rd Mon/6:30 p.m. Monthly	Anytime
Black Women's Literary Guild, Metro West Contact Person: Dana Johnson Address: 97 Hillside Ave. Concord, MA. 01742 Phone: (508) 369-5962 Fax: (508) 371-8875	1994	F	34	$15/yr	3rd Mon/6:30 p.m. Monthly	Anytime

Book Discussion Group	Year Founded	Membership Gender	No. of	Dues	Meeting Date/Time	Member Intake
Black Women's Literary Society Contact person: Rosalind Oliphant Address: 1806 Nueces St. Austin, TX 78701 Phone: (518) 478-5657	1993	F	50	$25/yr.	3rd Fri./ 6p.m. Monthly	Spring
BNN Booklovers Contact person: Angela Reid Address: 505 Kinard Dr. Winston-Salem, NC 27101 Phone (910) 723-5279	1966	M&F	20	N/A	Sat./6p.m. 6x/yr. Monthly	Anytime

Book Discussion Group	Year Founded	Membership Gender	No. of	Dues	Meeting Date/Time	Member Intake
The Book Club Contact person: James Watson-Akbar Address: 544-2 Gateway Blvd Boynton Beach, FL 33435 Phone: (407)731-4422 FAX: (407)731-0202	1994	M&F	10	N/A	Sat./5pm. Monthly	Anytime
Brothers & Sisters Contact person: Marsetta Lee Address: 150 Mercer St. #2A Trenton, NJ 08611 Phone: (609) 394-8517 Nationtime Bookstore 20% discount	1995	M&F	23	$10/yr	Sun./3 p.m.	Anytime

Book Discussion Group	Year Founded	Membership Gender	No. of	Dues	Meeting Date/Time	Member Intake
Bunch for Lunch Contact person: Jackie Caviel Address: 700 Louisiana Ste # 2200 Houston, TX 77002 Phone: (713) 220-8800 FAX: (713) 222-0843	1995	M&F	6	N/A	Monthly	Anytime
Community Book Forum Contact: K.O. Kushindana Address: Box 52916 Baton Rouge, LA. 70892-2916 Phone: (504) 356-0076 FAX: (504) 356-0076	1976	M&F	15	N/A	Sun/2 p.m. Monthly	Anytime

Book Discussion Group	Year Founded	Membership Gender	No. of	Dues	Meeting Date/Time	Member Intake
Ebony Esoterics Contact person: Annette Parks-Taylor Address: 2302 Tranquil Cove Ct Matthews, NC 28105 Phone: (704) 841-8695	1993	F	30	$2/yr	Sat./2:30 p.m. Monthly	Anytime
4th Monday Reading Group Contact person: Bernice Wiggins Address: 264 Willow Green Dr. Amherst, NY 14228 Phone: (716) 691-6183	1995	F	15	$1.00/yr	4th Mon./7 p.m. Monthly	Anytime

Book Discussion Group	Year Founded	Membership Gender	No. of	Dues	Meeting Date/Time	Member Intake
The Griot Society Contact person: Bonita M. Lockley Address: Box 34, College Station New York, NY 10030 Phone: (212) 926-5674	1994	M&F	20	5/mo.	Last Sun./4:30 p.m. Monthly	Anytime
The Imani Literary Reading Group Contact Person: Rashida Address: P.O. Box 1317 Atlanta, GA 30301 Phone: (770) 739-0905	1992	F	20	$2/mo.	Last Sat./1.p.m. Monthly	Anytime

Book Discussion Group	Year Founded	Membership Gender	No. of	Dues	Meeting Date/Time	Member Intake
Imani Nia Contact person: Clara Villarosa Address: 911 Park Ave. W Denver, CO 80205 Phone: (303)293-2665 FAX: (303)293-0046	1988	M&F	12	N/A	3rd Wed./6:30 p.m. Monthly	Anytime
Just Between Us Contact person: Lori Lewis Address: 324 Palmer St. Fredericksburg, VA., 22401-6119 Phone: (540) 373-5592 FAX: (202) 606-7495	1994	F	12	N/A	Every 6 wks. Fri./noon	When membership falls below 15

Book Discussion Group	Year Founded	Membership Gender	No. of	Dues	Meeting Date/Time	Member Intake
Ladies Literary Society Contact person: Rukayya Aksad Address: 6737 N. Wayne Rd. Westland, MI 48185 Phone: (313) 273-3733 FAX: (313) 273-5867	1992	F	16	$12./yr	Sun./5 p.m. Monthly	Anytime
The Literary Circle Contact Person: Nora Hudson Address: 18505 Plymouth Rd Detroit, MI 48228 Phone: (313) 272-5867 (313) 273-3733 Fax: (313) 273-5867	1988	F	31	N/A	Sun./3-6 p.m. Monthly	Invitation

Book Discussion Group	Year Founded	Membership Gender	No. of	Dues	Meeting Date/Time	Member Intake
Frances E.W. Harper Literary Society Contact person: Dorothea Moore Address: Box 25044 Newark, NJ 07101	1987	M&F	20	N/A	Wed./6:30 p.m. Monthly	Anytime
LNO (Ladies Night Out) Bookclub Contact person: Anita Johnson Address: 2303 Cranberry Terr Silver Spring, MD 20906 Phone: (301) 924-0451 FAX (301) 924-1955 E-mail anitahj@aol.com	1992	F	11	N/A	2nd Mon./6 p.m. Monthly	Anytime

Book Discussion Group	Year Founded	Membership Gender	No. of	Dues	Meeting Date/Time	Member Intake
Literary Sisters Contact person: Callie Crossley Address: MA Phone: (212)456-6944 (w/NYC) E-MARIAMMA@AOL.COM	1989	F	13	$10/yr.	Sun./3 p.m. Monthly	Invitation, once a yr.
Lorraine Hansbury Literary Club Contact person: DeBra Edwards Address: 7402 Palisades Hts. Ct. Houston, TX 77095 Phone: (713)758-2405 FAX: (713) 615-5034	1989	F	40	$1/meeting.	Sat./4 p.m. Bi-monthly	Anytime

Book Discussion Group	Year Founded	Membership Gender	No. of	Dues	Meeting Date/Time	Member Intake
Myrtle Literary Guild Contact person: Rosalind Johnson Address: 190 Temple St. W. Newton, MA 02165 Phone: (617)332-5704	1993	F	15	$5/yr	Sun./2 p.m. Monthly	Anytime
Oracle Set Book Club Contact: Virginia View Address: 516 Butternut St. N.W. Washington, DC 20012 Phone: (202)829-5929 (w) FAX: (202) 829-5929	1966	F	18	$10/yr.	4th Sun./4-6 p.m. Monthly	When membership falls below 18

Book Discussion Group	Year Founded	Membership Gender	No. of	Dues	Meeting Date/Time	Member Intake
The PALM Society Contact person: Beth Gibbs Address: 544 Simsbury Rd. Bloomfield, CT 06002 Phone: (860)242-6532 FAX: (860) 768-5016 E-gibbs@uhavax.hartford.edu	1991	F	16	$100/yr.	Sun./3 p.m. Monthly	Anytime
Pass It On Book Club Contact: Valaree Moodee Address: 8102 Highland Meadows Dr. Clinton, MD 20735 Phone: (301) 868-9639 FAX: (202) 752-5023 E-AlexII@AOL.com	1996	M&F	10	N/A	Sun./4 p.m. Monthly	Anytime

Book Discussion Group	Year Founded	Membership Gender	No. of	Dues	Meeting Date/Time	Member Intake
Positive Plus (Members, HIV-positive) (Reads and discusses own writing) Contact: Lauren Address: Center for Health & Living Whitman Walker Clinic 1407 S. St. NW Washington, DC Phone: (301) 589-2591	1995	M&F	10	N/A	Weekly	Anytime
The Reading Sisterhood Contact person: Beverly Braxon Cannon Address: 236 Custer Ave Newark, NJ 07112 Phone: (201) 923-7123	1993	F	13	$5/Meeting	8x/yr.	Periodically

Book Discussion Group	Year Founded	Membership Gender	No. of	Dues	Meeting Date/Time	Member Intake
Saturday Eves' Book Club	1968	F	20	$15/yr	Sat./7:30 p.m. Monthly	Anytime
Contact person: Gwen Etter-Lewis						
Address: 3387 Scotts Pine Way						
Kalamazoo, MI 49002						
S.I.L.K. (Sisters in Literary Kaleidescope)	1995	F	13	N/A	Thurs/Wed. 7 p.m. Monthly	Anytime
Contact person: Kimberly Jackson						
Address: 16939 Blend Stone						
Houston, TX 77084						
Phone: (713) 550-0674						

Book Discussion Group	Year Founded	Membership Gender	No. of	Dues	Meeting Date/Time	Member Intake
Takoma Mother-Daughter Book Club Daughter's age: 7–13 Contact person: Jenice View Address: 7008 9th St. NW Washington DC 20012 Phone: (202) 726-1942 FAX: (202)829-5929 E-Jenice@Aol.com	1996	F	8	N/A	Sun./2:30 p.m. Monthly	
You Go Girl African American Book Club Contact person: Jean Weathers Address: 2019 So. 21st Ave Broadview, IL 60153 Phone: (708) 531-7935 FAX: (708) 345-5416	1993	F	23	$5/yr	Sat./7 p.m. Quarterly	Anytime

Book
Sources

Where to Buy Them

AFRICAN AMERICAN IMAGES
(Mail Order)
1909 W. 95th St. S.E.
Chicago, IL 60643

AFRICAN HERITAGE LITERARY SOCIETY
(Mail Order)
1730 K St. N.W. Ste. 304
Washington, DC 20006

ARROYO BOOKS
(Spanish language, Latin American, Chicano)
125 S. Avenue 57
Los Angeles, CA 90042

BEYOND THE CLOSET
(Gay & Lesbian)
1501 Belmont Ave.
Seattle, WA 98122

BLACK BOOKS PLUS, INC.
(African-American)
702 Amsterdam Ave
New York, NY 10025

BLACK LITERARY CLUB
(Mail Order)
197 Prospect Pl.
Brooklyn, NY 11238

BLACKFEET COMMUNITY COLLEGE BOOKSTORE
(Native American)
Highway 2, Box 819
Browning, MT 59417

CHAPTER ONE
(Native American)
Box 790
Ketchum, ID 83340

CIRTULO de LECTORES
(Spanish-language/Mail Order)
(914) 534-4300

COMMUNITY BOOK FORUM
(African-American)
P.O. Box 52916
Baton Rouge, LA 70892

CULTURAL COLLECTIONS
(African-American)
754 Crescent St.
Brockton, MA 02402

DuSABLE MUSEUM BOOK STORE
(African-American)
740 E. 56th Pl.
Chicago, IL 60637

EASTWIND BOOKS & ARTS, INC.
(Chinese, Asian, Asian-American)
1435-A Stockton St.
San Francisco, CA 94133

FEMINIST BOOKSTORE NEWS
(Multi-cultural)
2358 Market St.
San Francisco, CA 94114-1521

FOLKTALES BOOKSTORE
(African-American)
1806 Nueces St.
Austin, TX 78701

GIOVANNI'S ROOM
(Gay & Lesbian)
345 S. 12th St.
Philadelphia, PA 19107-5907

HARVARD BOOKSTORE
(African, African-American, Asian-American, Latin Latino,
Middle-Eastern, Native American)
1258 Massachusetts Ave.
Cambridge, MA 02138

HUE-MAN EXPERIENCE
(African-American)
911-Park Avenue W.
Denver, CO 80205

JEONG EUM KOREN BOOK CENTER
928 So. Western Ave.
Korentown Plaza
Los Angeles, CA 90006

KINOKUNIYA BOOKSTORE
(Japanese)
10 W. 49th St.
New York, NY 10020

LECTORUM
(Spanish language)
137 W 14th St.
New York,

LI MIN BOOKS & STATIONERS
(Chinese)
969-N. Hill St.
Los Angeles, CA 90012

MANGAJIN BOOKSTORE
(Japanese)
Box 7119
Marietta, GA 30065-1119

NATIONAL ARCHIVES MUSEUM STORE
(Multicultural)
8th & Pennsylvania Ave. N.W.
Washington, DC, 20408

NEW WORDS BOOKSTORE
(Feminist/Multicultural)
186 Hampshire St.
Cambridge, MA 02139

ORIENTAL BOOKSTORE
(Asian, Mid-Eastern, Far-Eastern, Hawaiian, Asian-American)
1713 E. Colorado Blvd.
Pasadena, CA 91106

PRARIE EDGE TRADING CO. and GALLERIES
(Native American)
606 Main St.
Rapid City, SD 57701

RENAISSANCE BOOKS and COLLECTIBLES
(African American)
644 Massachusetts Ave., N.E.
Washington, DC 20002

SASUGA
(Japanese)
7 Upland Rd
Cambridge, MA
(617) 497-5460

SCHOENHOFS
(Foreign language books)
76A Mt. Auburn St.
Cambridge, MA 02138

SHRINE of the BLACK MADONNA
(African-American/African)
5309 Martin Luther King Blvd.
Houston, TX 77021

SHRINE of the BLACK MADONNA
(African-American/African)
13535 Livernois
Detroit, MI 48238

TREASURED LEGACY
(African-American)
100 Huntington Ave @ Copley Place
Boston, MA 02116

TUESDAY'S CHILD BOOKS
28 Hart Circle
Randolph, MA 02368

TUNDE DADA HOUSE OF AFRICA
356 Main St.
Orange, NJ 07050

ZANDBROZ
(Native American)
420 Broadway
Fargo, ND 58102

*Where To Find Out
What's Published*

AMERICAN BOOK REVIEW
University of Colorado at Bolder
Box 494
Bolder, CO 80309
(Guide to current books/ethnic)

BOOK WORLD
Washington Post Newspaper
Washington, DC 20071
(Book reviews)

BOOKWIRE WWW
http://www.bookwire.com/
(Lists author tour info, book reviews, best seller list)

BRAILLE BOOK REVIEW (Catalog)
Publications and Media Section
National Library Service for the Blind and Physically
Handicapped
Library of Congress
Washington, DC 20542
(Annotated book list)
or (For Large print catalog of books)
Friends of Libraries for Blind and Handicapped Individuals
155 Connecticut Ave. N.W., Ste 200
Washington D.C. 20036

EL JUGLAR
University of Maryland
College Park, MD 20742
(Literary magazine)

EXITO: MAGAZINE FOR ALL FILIPINOS
News and Sun Sentinel Co #212
8323 NW 12th St.
Miami, FL 33126
(Reviews and Interviews)

HIGH PLAINS LITERARY REVIEW
180 Adams St. Ste. 250
U. of Colorado Health Science Ctr.
Denver, CO 80206
(Book reviews, ethnic focus)

NATIVE PEOPLES MAGAZINE
5333 N 7th St. Ste.C-224
Phoenix, AZ 85014
(Book excerpts)

RAWI
(Radius of Arab-American Writers, Inc.)
Box 620, Prince St. Station
New York, NY 10012

Si (Latino)
Box 36559
Los Angeles, CA 90099
(Books, interviews, articles)

QBR
(Quarterly Black Review)
625 Broadway 10th Flr
New York, NY 10012
Books, interviews, articles

WINDSPEAKER:
Aboriginal Multi-Media Society of Alberta
15001 112th Avenue
Edmonton, Alberta T5M2V6 Canada
(403) 455-2700
(Native American, books, interviews, profiles)

My book discussion group diary

NAME OF GROUP _____

BOOK _____DATE READ _____

AUTHOR _____

PUBLISHER _____DATE PUB. _____

OTHER BOOKS BY AUTHOR	DATE PUB.	DATE READ
_____	_____	_____
_____	_____	_____
_____	_____	_____
_____	_____	_____
_____	_____	_____
_____		

NOTES/COMMENTS _____

_____

_____

_____

_____

_____

_____

RECOMMEND: YES / NO,

COMMENTS _____

RATING I GIVE THIS BOOK_____

RATING DISCUSSION GROUP GAVE BOOK _____

RATING I GIVE THE AUTHOR _____

RATING DISCUSSION GROUP GAVE AUTHOR _____

BOOK LOANED TO: DATE   RET'D

_____   _____   _____

_____   _____   _____

_____   _____   _____

_____   _____   _____

Book Rating

- 5 Points
  Would read again and can't wait to recommend to a friend
- 4 Points
  Wouldn't read again, but would give as a gift
- 3 Points
  Just okay
- 2 Points
  Would rather wait for video
- 1 Points
  Didn't like it enough to read past page ten.